golden

understanding and caring for your breed

Written by
Matthew Burns

Dog Expert | 1

golden retriever

understanding and
caring for your breed

Written by
Matthew Burns

Pet Book Publishing Company

St. Martin's Farm, Zeals, Warminster, BA12 6NP, United Kingdom.

Printed by Printworks Global Ltd., London & Hong Kong

All rights reserved. No part of this work may be reproduced, in any form or by any means, electronic or mechanical, including photocopying, recording or by any information storage and retrieval system, without the prior written permission of the publisher.

Copyright © Pet Book Publishing Company 2014.

Every reasonable care has been taken in the compilation of this publication. The Publisher and Author cannot accept liability for any loss, damage, injury or death resulting from the keeping of Golden Retrievers by user(s) of this publication, or from the use of any materials, equipment, methods or information recommended in this publication or from any errors or omissions that may be found in the text of this publication or that may occur at a future date, except as expressly provided by law.

The 'he' pronoun is used throughout this book instead of the rather impersonal 'it', however no gender bias is intended.

ISBN: 978-1-906305-82-6
ISBN: 1-906305-82-X

Acknowledgements

The publishers would like to thank the following for help with photography: Kim Ellis (Tenfield)

Contents

Introducing the Golden Retriever	8
Tracing back in time	16
Developing the breed	20
What should a Golden Retriever look like?	24
What do you want from your Goldie?	34
What does your Goldie want from you?	38
Extra considerations	44
Male or female?	44
More than one?	47
An older dog	48
Rehoming a rescued dog	50
Sourcing a puppy	52
Puppy watching	60
A Goldie-friendly home	68
Settling in	82
House training	94
Choosing a diet	98
Caring for your Goldie	106
Social skills	122
Training guidelines	130
First lessons	134
Come when called	140
Stationary exercises	144

Control exercises	148
Opportunities for Goldies	154
Health care	162
Common ailments	174
Breed-specific disorders	182

Introducing the Golden Retriever

Loyal, loving, intelligent and stunning to look at, the Golden Retriever is a superb family companion with a worldwide fan club. Once you have owned a Goldie, no other breed will do...

The Golden Retriever was developed as a top-class gundog, capable of using initiative, yet always biddable to his master. It is this combination of intelligence and willingness that makes the breed so special.

Physical characteristics

The first impression of the Golden Retriever is one of energy and athleticism. He was bred as a working dog, and retains the powerful, active build of a dog

that has speed, endurance and agility. Balance and symmetry are the words that best describe his conformation, and when he moves with long, effortless strides, he is a joy to behold.

The Golden Retriever has a broad, finely-chiseled head, framed by drop ears that are set level with his eyes. The typical expression is alert and intelligent, but the dark brown eyes offer something more. They are soft and melting and seem almost like a mirror on the soul of this wonderful breed.

The topline – the line along the back – is firm and straight, ending in the feathered tail, which is carried level with the back when a dog is on the move. This is very important as it gives the Golden Retriever his very distinctive look; he exudes self-confidence, optimism and gaiety.

The coat can be wavy or flat; the most important feature for a working gundog is for it to be weatherproof, and therefore the dense undercoat is essential. The colour is, of course, golden, but this does not mean the breed lacks variety. The shades range from the very palest cream to a rich, lustrous golden. The black pigment on the nose and eye-rims provide a dramatic contrast and are very much a breed feature.

Temperament

Where to start? The Golden Retriever has an outstanding temperament which makes him the ideal working dog and the perfect companion. He is intelligent and can think for himself, but he remains biddable so he will take direction. He is exceptionally sweet-natured and relates well to people of all ages. He loves children, combing the roles of nanny and playmate with kindly ease.

Occasionally his halo will slip: the Golden Retriever does have a stubborn side, but this is easily circumnavigated if you are a little creative with your training. The good-tempered Goldie reacts best to positive methods; make something sufficiently rewarding and he will be back to his best, tail wagging and eager to co-operate.

Breed characteristcs

The Golden Retriever has a number of specialities which are very much part of his charm.

Bred to retrieve, the Goldie takes this role very seriously and is never happier than when he has something in his mouth. It really doesn't matter what it is – a toy, a book, a shoe, a tea towel – all are regarded as suitable gifts to present to you when you return home, or to welcome unsuspecting visitors.

Golden Retrievers love being included in family outings, and many Goldies view the car with special affection. It is a positive treat for a Golden Retriever to be taken on a car trip, even if it is no more than going to the shops and back. If the car is in the drive with the back open, you can bet your Goldie will take up pole position...

The beautiful golden coat is one of the stunning aspects of the breed but, unfortunately, few Goldies take a pride in their appearance. A Goldie likes water and mud, and a combination of both is best of all. You can set off on a walk on a dry, sunny day, but somehow you always return with a dirty, dishevelled Goldie, who appears highly delighted with his makeover...

Facing page: What a Goldie wants most is to be a part of all family activities.

Lifestyle choices

The Golden Retriever is a medium-sized dog with an adaptable outlook on life and, as such, he is a good choice for a range of different owners.

He will be a cheerful and loving family companion, and thrives on being included in all activities. But he will also suit older, active owners and will form a close bond with the special people in his life.

Although essentially a country dog, he will be perfectly happy in an urban setting as long as he is given sufficient exercise.

But there is one aspect of Golden Retriever ownership that is non-negotiable. This is a breed that thrives on human companionship, and if you have to spend long periods at work, and will be forced to leave your Goldie home alone, you should definitely think again. No breed of dog should be left for lengthy periods, but a Goldie, more than most, regards separation as pure torture.

This is a most adaptable breed but a Goldie will be miserable if he is faced with lengthy periods on his own.

Dog Expert | 15

Tracing back in time

The history of many dog breeds is shrouded in mystery, and it is difficult to separate fact from fiction, myth from reality. However, the Golden Retriever has a remarkably well-documented history which traces back to a country estate in Scotland.

Talent spotting

The first Lord Tweedsmouth, the owner of Guisachan, a 20,000 acre estate in Inverness-shire, wanted to develop his own line of working dogs that were suitable for hunting and retrieving game on his land.

One day, he was walking along the streets of Brighton and he spotted a dog called Nous, the only yellow dog in a litter of black Wavy Coated Retrievers, bred by Lord Chichester. Lord

Facing page: The fifth Earl of Illchester, pictured with Ada, 1875

Tweedsmouth knew instantly that this was the type of dog he had been searching for. He negotiated a price with Lord Chichester and took Nous back to Scotland with him.

In 1868 he started his breeding programme by mating Nous with Belle, a Tweed Water Spaniel from the Ladykirk area on the River Tweed. The result was three yellow puppies, a male named Crocus, and two females, Cowslip and Primrose. These puppies were to be the foundation of the Golden Retriever breed; we have detailed knowledge of how the breed evolved in the early days thanks to the meticulous record-keeping of Lord Tweedsmouth.

Artistocratic connections

Lord Tweedsmouth kept Cowslip and Primrose at Guisachan and he gave Crocus to his son (later the second Lord Tweedsmouth). A second litter by Nous and Belle produced Ada, given to Lord Tweedsmouth's nephew, the fifth Earl of Ilchester, who started the Ilchester line of Golden Retrievers.

Lord Tweedmouth continued his breeding programme using the offspring of Nous and Belle, sometimes introducing fresh blood, such as outcrossing to a Tweed Water Spaniel and later to an Irish Setter. It is also thought that a Bloodhound may have been added to the mix.

American link

When Lord Tweedmouth's youngest son, the Hon. Archie Marjoribanks, went to America to run the family ranch in Texas, he took a Golden Retriever, called Sol, with him. There are no records available, but there is a photo taken in the early 1890s of Archie Marjoribanks sitting astride a horse, with a Golden Retriever, called Lady, by his side. It is thought that Sol was the sire of Lady, but what is certain is that Lady went on to be the foundation bitch for the breed in the USA. Further imports from the UK in the first half of the Twentieth century ensured its success.

Developing the breed

It did not take long for news of the 'new' breed to spread outside Scotland, and in the early 1900s a number of pioneers adopted the Golden Retriever as their chosen breed.

Influential dogs

The first Champion of the breed was Noranby Campfire, who was sired by Lord Harcourt's Culham Copper out of a bitch called Noranby Beauty, owned by Mrs Charlesworth. Both the Culham and the Noranby kennels went on to have a significant influence on the development of the breed.

At this stage, the Golden Retriever was equally prized for his prowess in the field, exemplified by Michael of Moreton. Highly successful in Field Trials, he was campaigned in the show ring and went on to win more Challenge Certificates than any other

Facing page: Intelligent and biddable, the Golden Retriever can be trained for many different roles, including the vital work of search and rescue.

Golden Retriever prior to World War Two. He was a prolific sire and had a huge impact on the breed.

The great divide

But the days of dual purpose Golden Retrievers which could excel in the show ring and in the shooting field are now long gone. Over the years, sporting enthusiasts pursued the type that was most suited to hunting and retrieving while the show people focused on producing dogs that adhered to the stipulations of the Breed Standard (see What Should A Golden Retriever Look Like, page 24). It is the show-bred Golden Retrievers that we usually find as pets.

The working Golden Retriever is finer in build and longer in the leg than his show cousin, as he is primarily bred for speed and athleticism. Show dogs are heavier and squarer in build; they may have a broader head and their coats will have more feathering. Working Goldens are often darker, sometimes almost red in colour.

In terms of temperament, both types share the same friendly, confident nature, but working Goldens need more exercise and mental stimulation.

All rounders

The Golden Retriever is now well established the world over as a glamorous show dog, a brilliant working gundog, a talented competitor in canine sports, and an outstanding companion dog. But this is not the end of the breed's achievements.

The character and conformation of the Golden Retriever makes him an ideal candidate for working as an assistance dog. First chosen as a guide dog, he is now widely used with both adults and children with physical disabilities. He is highly successful as a hearing dog for deaf people, he is one of the breeds used as a seizure alert dog, and has also been trained as a companion for autistic children.

If that was not enough, the Golden Retriever has also made his mark as a sniffer dog, working with Customs, the police and the armed forces to find arms, explosives and drugs. He is also a brilliant search and rescue dog and has done invaluable work finding survivors in the wake of major disasters such as earthquakes and terrorist attacks.

Lord Tweedsmouth was inspired by the idea of establishing his own line of working retrievers; in fact he masterminded a breed that has a truly global following.

What should a Golden Retriever look like?

> With his powerful, symmetrical body, his glorious coat and his intelligent, kindly expression, The Golden Retriever draws admiring glances wherever he goes. So what makes a Goldie so special?

The aim of breeders is to produce dogs that are sound, healthy, typical examples of their chosen breed, in terms of both looks and temperament To achieve this, they are guided by a Breed Standard, which is a written blueprint describing what the perfect specimen should look like.

Of course, there is no such thing as a 'perfect' dog, but breeders aspire to produce dogs that conform as closely as possible to the picture in words presented by the Breed Standard. In the show ring, judges use the Breed Standard to assess the dogs that come before them, and

it is the dog that, in their opinion, comes closest to the ideal, that will win top honours.

This has significance beyond the sport of showing for it is the dogs that win in the ring that will be used for breeding. The winners of today are therefore responsible for passing on their genes to future generations and preserving the breed in its best form.

There are some differences in the wording of the Breed Standard depending on national Kennel Clubs; the American Standard is certainly more descriptive than the English version and gives you a better idea of what the breed should really look like.

General appearance

This is essentially a working dog and should appear active, sound and well put together, with no hint of clumsiness. His balance, gait and purpose should be valued beyond his component parts.

Temperament

The Golden Retriever is loved the world over for his superb temperament. This is a confident dog that is kindly and friendly with everyone he meets. He is entirely trustworthy, and his biddable, intelligent nature makes him a first class worker as well as being a loving family companion.

Points of anatomy

Head and skull

Balance is an essential ingredient in the make-up of the Golden Retriever and this applies to the head which must be in balance with the body. The distinction between males and females should be instantly discernible from the head.

The skull is broad and well chiseled, without coarseness; the muzzle is wide and powerful and blends smoothly into the skull. The stop (the step between the muzzle and the foreface) is well defined but not abrupt. The length of the foreface should equal the length from the stop to the occiput (the back part of the skull).

Dark pigment is a feature of the breed, so the nose should be black, although it may fade to a lighter shade in cold weather.

Eyes

The eyes are medium-sized and set well apart with dark, close-fitting rims. They should be dark brown in colour and, most importantly, they should convey an impression of kindliness and intelligence.

Ears

The ears are moderate in size ('rather short' according to the American Breed Standard), but when pulled forward the tip of the ear should cover the eye. They are set on a level with the eyes.

Mouth

As a working retriever, the Goldie must have powerful jaws and a soft mouth to carry game unharmed back to his handler. The teeth should meet in a perfect scissor bite with the teeth on the upper jaw closely overlapping the teeth on the lower jaw. The American Standard states that an undershot bite (the teeth on the lower jaw protruding in front of the teeth on the upper jaw) or an overshot bite (when the teeth on the upper jaw protrude beyond the teeth on the lower jaw) should serve as a disqualification in the show ring.

Neck

The neck should be of good length; it should be clean and muscular, merging gradually into well laid-back shoulders.

Forequarters

The front legs are straight with good bone; the shoulder blades are long, equal in length to the upper arm, which places the legs well under the body. The elbows should be close fitting.

Body

The body is balanced and short coupled, and is deep through the heart. The ribs are well sprung, and the topline – the line from shoulders to tail – is strong and level.

Hindquarters

The hindquarters should be broad, strong and muscular. The stifle (the knee joint) is well bent and the hocks (ankle joints) should be straight when viewed from the rear, neither turning in nor out.

Feet

The feet are round and cat-like; they should be compact and well knuckled with thick pads.

Tail

The tail completes the picture of balance in the Golden Retriever, so it is essential that it is carried correctly.

It needs to be well set on and muscular at the base, following a natural line from the croup (rump). When a Golden Retriever is moving, the tail is carried level with the back. The American Standard allows for a moderate upward curve, but a gay tail which curls over the back is heavily penalised.

Facing page: Colour ranges from pale cream to deep golden.

Coat

There are two types of coat: flat (straight) and wavy. However both must have a dense, water-repellent undercoat. The topcoat should be firm and resilient, lying close to the body. The ruff is natural and untrimmed and there should be moderate feathering on the back of the front legs and underbody, with heavier feathering on the front of the neck, the back of the thighs and the underside of the tail.

Colour

There is a beautiful range of shades ranging from gold to cream. Goldens from working lines are often darker in colour, which is not so desirable in show dogs. In fact the UK Standard specifically states that red or mahogany is not acceptable, whereas the American Standard asks for the colours to be 'rich, lustrous golden of various shades.'

In the UK, Goldens may be so pale in colour as to be near white, but this is rarely seen in the USA.

Movement

A Golden Retriever in full flow looks magnificent with his free, easy stride. He should show good drive, and be straight and true both front and rear.

Size

There is a slight difference in the stipulations for height between the American and UK Standards.

The UK Standard asks for males to be 56 to 61cm (22 to 24in) at the shoulder and bitches to be 51 to 56cm (20 to 22in).

The American Standard asks for males to be 58 to 61cm (23 to 24in) and females to be 55 to 57cm (21.5-22.5 in). In addition, the American Standard states that Goldens more than one inch above or below the standard size should be disqualified in the show ring.

Summing up

Although the majority of Golden Retrievers are kept as pet dogs or working dogs and will never be exhibited in the show ring, it is important that breeders strive for perfection and try to produce dogs that adhere as closely as possible to the Breed Standard. This is the best way of ensuring that the Goldie remains sound in mind and body, and retains the characteristics that are unique to this very special breed.

What do you want from your Goldie?

There are hundreds of dog breeds to choose from, so how can you be sure that the Golden Retriever is the right breed for you? Before you take the plunge into Goldie ownership, you need to be 100 per cent confident that this is the breed that is best suited to your lifestyle.

Companion

If you want an intelligent good-looking, affectionate family pet, look no further. Gundogs are blessed with being exceptionally sound in both mind and body, and the Golden Retriever excels as a reliable and trustworthy companion.

He is intelligent and engaging, and has his own sense of humour which can be highly entertaining. As far as the Golden Retriever is concerned, life is for the living; as a youngster he hurls himself into family life and although he may become a little more sedate as he gets older, he never loses his boundless enthusiasm.

He also has a softer, sensitive side and seems to 'tune in' to his people, reflecting their moods, and providing fun, companionship and love whenever it is needed.

Working gundog

Golden Retrievers from working lines make excellent gundogs, specialising in retrieving on land and from water. A hardy, resilient dog, the working Goldie will work tirelessly, running out with zest for every retrieve until the sun sets on the shooting field.

Sports dog

This is a breed that thrives on having a job to do and Golden Retrievers have proved themselves in all the canine sports. A good nose and an independent mind are invaluable for tracking and working trials, a biddable, co-operative nature responds to the precision required in obedience, an active body and quick-thinking brain makes for an excellent agility competitor, and the flair and good looks of a Goldie makes him a star turn in canine freestyle.

Show dog

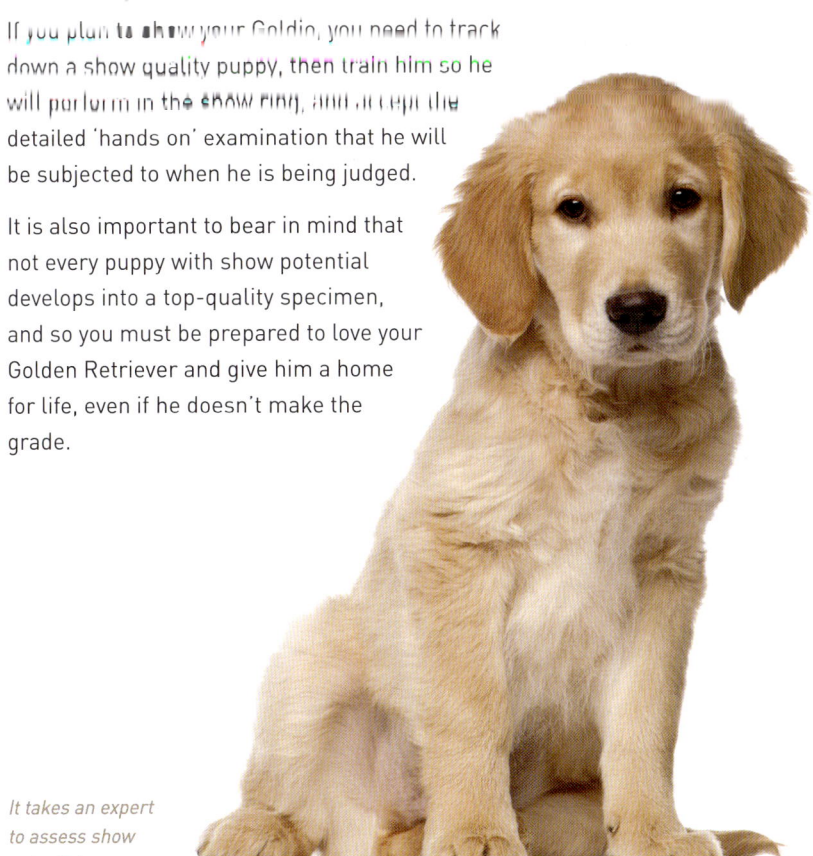

If you plan to show your Goldie, you need to track down a show quality puppy, then train him so he will perform in the show ring, and accept the detailed 'hands on' examination that he will be subjected to when he is being judged.

It is also important to bear in mind that not every puppy with show potential develops into a top-quality specimen, and so you must be prepared to love your Golden Retriever and give him a home for life, even if he doesn't make the grade.

It takes an expert to assess show potential.

What does your Goldie want from you?

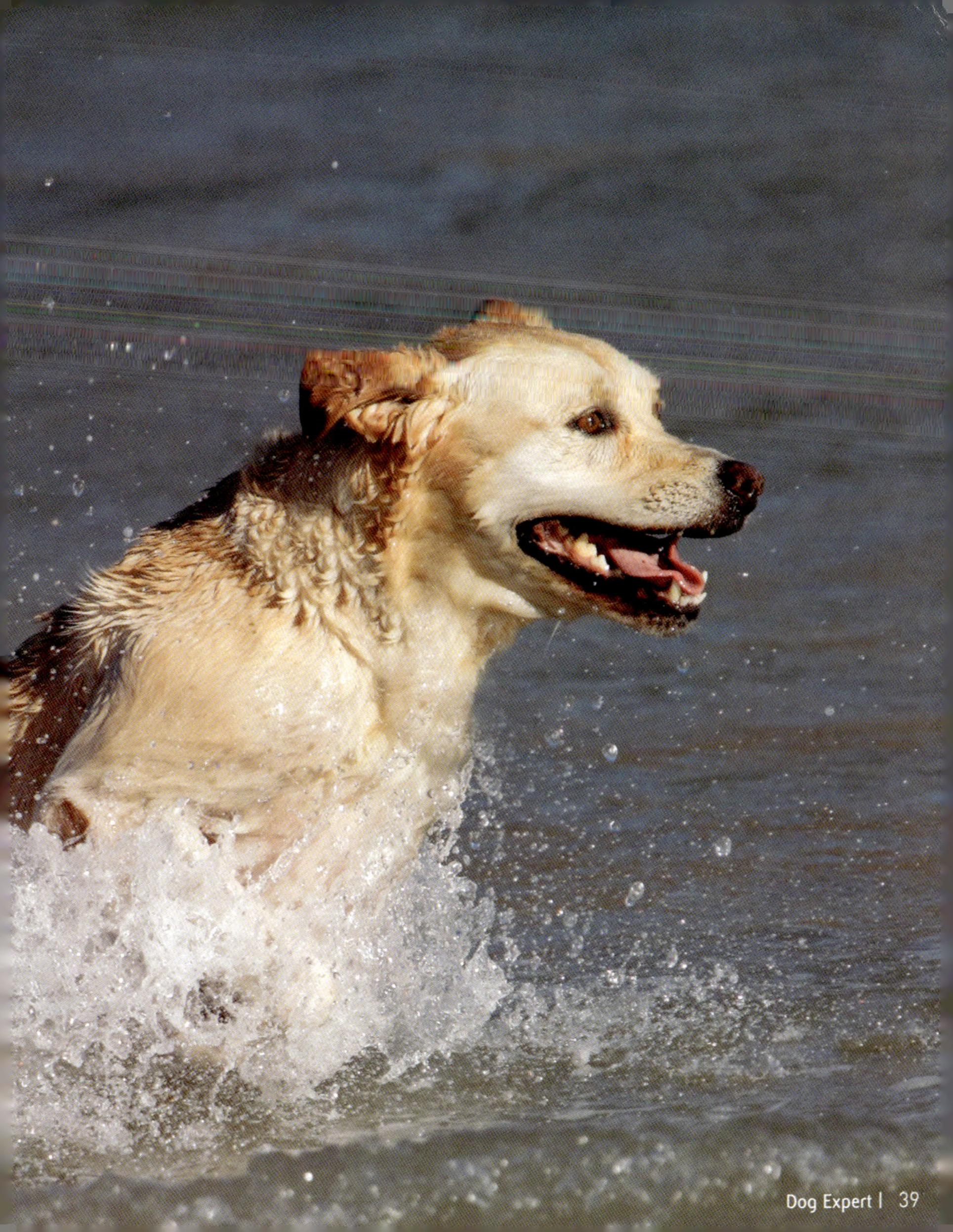

A dog cannot speak for himself, so we need to view the world from a canine perspective and work out what a Golden Retriever needs in order to live a happy, contented and fulfilling life.

Time and commitment

First of all, a Golden Retriever needs a commitment that you will care for him for the duration of his life – guiding him through his puppyhood, enjoying his adulthood, and being there for him in his later years. If all potential owners were prepared to make this pledge, there would be scarcely any dogs in rescue.

The Golden Retriever was bred to be a working gundog and although he has become a companion dog *par excellence*, it is important to remember that he has a brain and he needs to use it. A bored Goldie will invent mischief of his own, becoming destructive or developing other behavioural problems, if left to his own devices.

It is also important to bear in mind that the Golden Retriever is very much a 'people dog', and he may react very badly if he is left for lengthy periods on his own. A dog should never be left for longer than four hours at a stretch, and if you cannot fulfil this obligation, you would be wise to delay taking on a dog of any breed until your situation changes.

Although spending time with your Golden Retriever is a top priority, you also need to teach him to cope with spending time on his own. Goldies can become very needy and experience separation anxiety, if they are not accustomed to coping with time spent alone.

From puppyhood, make sure your Goldie spends some time on his own, preferably in a crate where he will feel safe and secure. Do not make a fuss when you leave him and, equally important, do not make a fuss when you return. Being left should be seen as a matter of routine so your Goldie is confident in the knowledge that you go – but you always come back again.

Practical matters

The Golden Retriever is very much a middle of the road dog when it comes to care. He is not so big as to need a huge house and a large car, but neither is he a handy side that will fit all situations. With a Golden Retriever, you certainly know you have dog in the family, and males, in particular, can make their presence felt!

The Golden Retriever does not have the easy, low maintenance coat of a breed such as the Labrador

Retriever, but he does not require the high maintenance grooming required for long-coated breeds.

In terms of exercise, a Golden Retriever is more demanding. He needs the opportunity to use his body – walking, running, swimming and investigating scents – come rain or shine.

Leadership

The Golden Retriever is one of the most amiable of breeds and, for the most part, he is eager to please. However, he does have a mind of his own, and may become demanding in his behaviour if he does not know where the boundaries lie. This is most likely to occur during adolescence, when it is natural for males, in particular, to flex their muscles.

It is your job to provide leadership – not by crushing your dog's spirit, but by encouraging the behaviour you want using praise and rewards. Be consistent in everything you do and your Goldie will understand what is required of him and will feel at ease with his place in the family pack.

A contented Goldie will be happy to abide by the family rules.

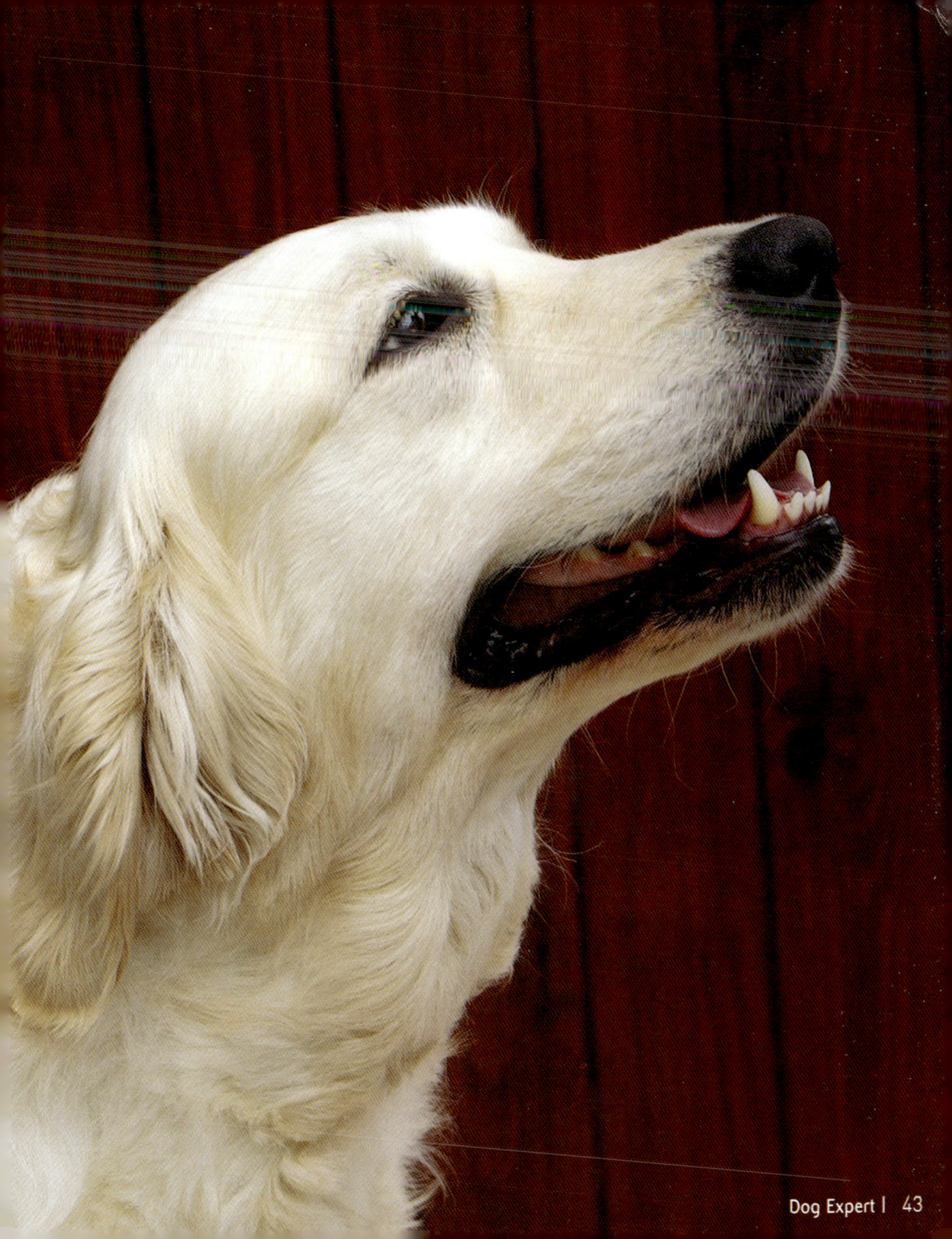

Extra considerations

Now you have decided that a Golden Retriever is the dog of your dreams, you can narrow your choice so you know exactly what you are looking for.

Male or female?

The choice of whether you get a male or female Goldie comes down to personal preference. Some claim that males are more loving and loyal; others say females are always sweet natured and affectionate. There is also a contingent that recognises the 'princess' nature of some female Goldies – but that is very much part of their charm!

In point of fact, there is little to choose between the male/female temperaments; it is the character of the Golden Retriever that is outstanding so you will be delighted with either sex.

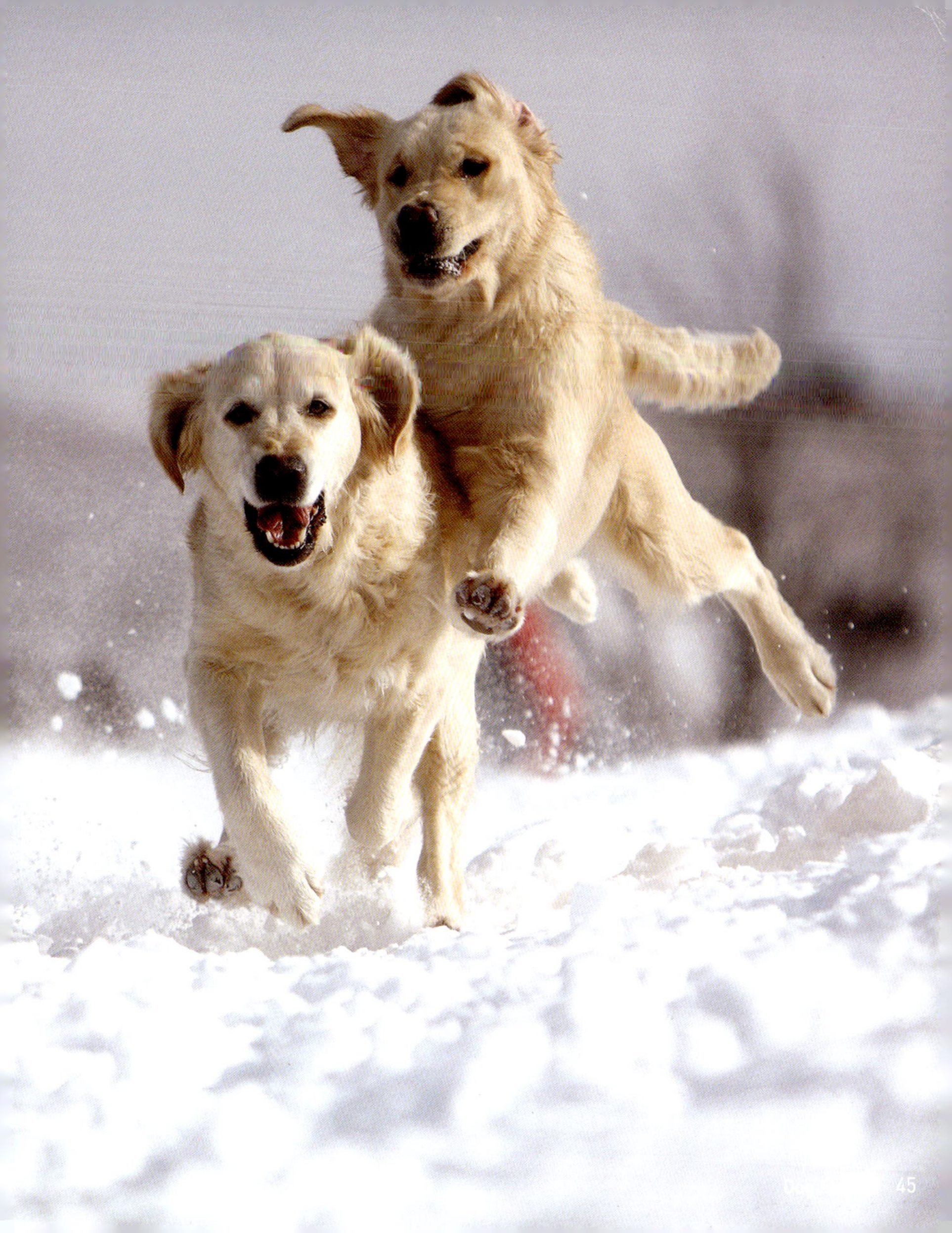

The male is a bigger, heavier animal. He may be a little more boisterous, particularly during adolescence, but if you instill good manners from an early age, this should not be difficult to manage.

If you opt for a female, you will need to cope with her seasons, which will start at around seven to eight months of age and occur approximately every nine months. During the three-week period of a season, you will need to keep your bitch away from entire males (males that have not been neutered) to eliminate the risk of an unwanted pregnancy. Some owners report that females may be a little moody and withdrawn.

Many pet owners opt for neutering, which puts an end to the seasons, and also and has many attendant health benefits. The operation, known as spaying, is usually carried out at some point after the first season. The best plan is to seek advice from your vet.

An entire male may not cause many problems, although some do have a stronger tendency to mark, which could include the house. However, training will usually put a stop to this. An entire male will also be on the lookout for bitches in season, and this may lead to difficulties, depending on your circumstances.

Neutering (castrating) a male is a relatively simple operation, and there are associated health benefits. Again, you should seek advice from your vet.

More than one?

Golden Retriever pups are utterly gorgeous, but even if you decide you would like to have two dogs in your family, do not fall into the trap of getting two puppies from the same litter, or even two of a similar age.

The two puppies will have no problem with the plan; they will always have someone to play with. But this could be at the cost of forming a proper bond with members of their human family.

You also need to consider the effect that rearing two puppies will have on your life. Looking after one puppy is hard work, but taking on two pups at the same time is more than double the workload. House training is a nightmare as, often, you don't even know which puppy is making mistakes, and training is impossible unless you separate the two puppies and give them one-on-one attention.

Resist the temptation of taking on two puppies.

Be very wary of a breeder who encourages you to buy two puppies from the same litter, as it is unlikely that the welfare of the puppies is their top priority. Most responsible breeders have a waiting list of potential purchasers before a litter is even born and have no need to make this type of sale.

If you do decide to add to your Goldie population, wait at least 18 months so your first dog is fully trained and settled before taking on a puppy.

An older dog

You may decide to miss out on the puppy phase and take on an older dog instead. Such a dog may be harder to track down, but sometimes a breeder may have a youngster that is not suitable for showing, but is perfect as a family pet. In some cases, a breeder may rehome a female when her breeding career is at an end so she will enjoy the benefits of more individual attention.

There are advantages to taking on an older dog, as you know exactly what you are getting. But the upheaval of changing homes can be quite upsetting, so you will need to have plenty of patience during the settling in period.

It may suit your lifestyle to take on an adult dog

Dog Expert | 49

Rehoming a rescued dog

We are fortunate that the number of Golden Retrievers that end up in rescue is still relatively small as Goldies are such an easy-going breed, but inevitably there are a few that find their way there.

In most cases, a Golden Retriever ends up in rescue through no fault of his own. The reasons are various, ranging from illness or death of the original owner to family breakdown, changing jobs, or even the arrival of a new baby.

You may find a Goldie in an all-breed rescue centre, but you will probably find that contacting a specialist breed club that runs a rescue scheme will be your best option if you decide to go down this route.

Try to find out as much as you can about a dog's history so you know exactly what you are taking on. You need to be aware of his age and health status, his likes and dislikes, plus any behavioural issues that may be relevant. You need to be realistic about what you are capable of achieving so you can be sure you can give the dog in question a permanent home.

Again, you need to give a rescued Goldie plenty of time and patience as he settles into his new home, but if all goes well, you will have the reward of knowing that you have given your dog a second chance.

Can you offer a Goldie a second chance to find a forever home?

Dog Expert | 51

Sourcing a puppy

Your aim is to find a healthy puppy that is typical of the breed, and has been reared with the greatest possible care. Where do you start?

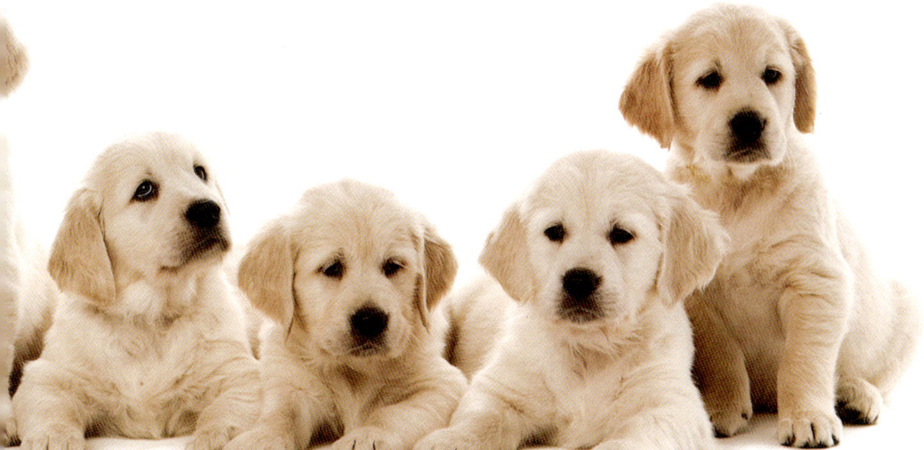

A tried-and-trusted method of finding a puppy is to attend a dog show where your chosen breed is being exhibited. This will give you the opportunity to see lots of different Golden Retrievers. You will notice the different shades of Goldies, and the difference between the flat and wavy coat. But when you look closely, you will also see there are different 'types' on show. They are all purebred Golden Retrievers, but breeders produce dogs with a family likeness, so you can see which type you prefer.

When judging has been completed, talk to the exhibitors and find out more about their dogs. They may not have puppies available, but some will be planning a litter, and you may decide to put your name on a waiting list.

Internet research

The Internet is an excellent resource, but when it comes to finding a puppy, use it with care:

DO go to the website of your national Kennel Club.

Both the American Kennel Club (AKC) and the Kennel Club (KC) have excellent websites which will give you information about the Golden Retriever as a breed, and what to look for when choosing a puppy. You will also find contact details for specialist breed clubs (see opposite).

Both sites have lists of puppies available, and you can look out for breeders of merit (AKC) and assured breeders (KC) which indicates that a code of conduct has been adhered to.

To find details of specialist breed clubs.

On breed club websites you will find lots of useful information which will help you to care for your Goldie. There may be contact details of breeders in your area, or you may need to go through the club secretary. Some websites also have a list of breeders that have puppies available. The advantage of going through a breed club is that members will follow a code of ethics, and this will give you some guarantees regarding breeding stock and health checks.

If you are planning to show your Golden Retriever you will obviously go to a breeder that specialises in show lines. This may also be the best source if you want a Goldie purely as a companion, as show-bred dogs are generally a little less demanding in terms of what they need regarding exercise and mental stimulation. But if you are planning to work your Goldie in the field, or you are a serious agility competitor, you should focus on breeders that produce working lines.

DO NOT look at puppies for sale.

There are legitimate Golden Retriever breeders with their own websites, and they may, occasionally, advertise a litter, although in most cases reputable breeders have waiting lists for their puppies. The danger comes from unscrupulous breeders that produce puppies purely for profit, with no thought for the health of the dogs they breed from and no care given to rearing the litter. Photos of puppies are hard to resist, but never make a decision based purely on an advertisement. You need to find out who the breeder is, and have the opportunity to visit their premises and inspect the litter before making a decision.

Questions, questions, questions

When you find a breeder with puppies available, you will have lots of questions to ask. These should include the following:

- Where have the puppies been reared? Hopefully, they will be in a home environment which gives them the best possible start in life.

- How many are in the litter?

- What is the split of males and females?

- How many have already been spoken for? The

breeder will probably be keeping a puppy to show or for breeding, and there may be others on a waiting list.

- Can I see the mother with her puppies?
- What age are the puppies?
- When will they be ready to go to their new homes?

Bear in mind puppies need to be with their mother and siblings until they are eight weeks of age otherwise they miss out on vital learning and communication skills which will have a detrimental effect on them for the rest of their lives.

You should also be prepared to answer a number of searching questions so the breeder can check if you are suitable as a potential owner of one of their precious puppies.

It is important to see the mother with her puppies.

You will be asked some or all of the following questions:

- What is your home set up?
- Do you have children/grandchildren?
- What are their ages?
- Is there somebody at home the majority of the time?
- What is your previous experience with dogs?
- Do you have plans to show or work your Golden Retriever?

The breeder is not being intrusive; they need to understand the type of home you will be able to provide in order to make the right match. Do not be offended by this; the breeder is doing it for both the dog's benefit and also for yours.

Steer clear of a breeder who does not ask you questions. He or she may be more interested in making money out of the puppies rather than ensuring that they go to good homes. They may also have taken other short cuts which may prove disastrous, and very expensive, in terms of vet bills or plain heartache.

Health issues

In common with all purebred dogs, the Golden Retriever suffers from some hereditary problems so you need to talk to the breeder about the health status of breeding stock and find out if there are any issues of concern. There are health clearances for hip dysplasia and some eye disorders, which should have been carried out, with the relevant paperwork available to view.

For information on inherited conditions, see page 182.

Your aim is to find a healthy puppy that is typical of the breed.

Puppy watching

Golden Retriever puppies are totally irresistible; they look like wooly teddy bears, and when you see a litter you will want to take the whole lot home with you! However, you must try to put your feelings to one side so that you can make an informed choice. You need to be 100 per cent confident that the breeding stock is healthy, and the puppies have been reared with love and care, before making a commitment to buy.

Viewing a litter

It is a good idea to have mental checklist of what to look out for when you visit a breeder. You want to see:

- A clean, hygienic environment.

- Puppies who are out-going and friendly, and eager to meet you.

Dog Expert | 61

- A sweet-natured mother who is ready to show off her puppies.

- Puppies that are well covered, but not pot-bellied, which could be an indication of worms.

- Bright eyes, with no sign of soreness or discharge.

- Clean ears that smell fresh.

- No discharge from the nose.

- Clean rear ends – matting could indicate upset tummies.

- Lively pups that are keen to play.

It is important that you see the mother with her puppies as this will give you a good idea of the temperament they are likely to inherit. It is also helpful if you can see other close relatives so you can see the type of Golden Retriever the breeder produces.

In most cases, you will not be able to see the father (sire) as most breeders will travel some distance to find a stud dog that is not too close to their own bloodlines and complements their bitch. However, you should be able to see photos of him and be given the chance to examine his pedigree and show record.

Companion puppy

If you are looking for a Goldie as a companion, you should be guided by the breeder who will have spent hours and hours puppy watching, and will know each of the pups as individuals. It is tempting to choose a puppy yourself, but the breeder will take into account your family set up and lifestyle, and will help you to pick the most suitable puppy.

Look for a confident puppy who is keen to greet you.

Dog Expert | 63

Working puppy

The Golden Retriever is highly prized as a working gundog, and breeders produce dogs specifically for this discipline, using breeding lines going back over many generations to dogs that have shown the important attributes for working in the field.

As already highlighted, working Golden Retrievers do look noticeably different from show-bred Goldies, and they also have a more driven outlook on life.

If you plan to work your Golden Retriever, make your intentions clear to the breeder who will help you with your choice and may well provide advice on rearing and training strategies.

Sports puppy

If you are looking for a puppy to compete in one of the canine sports, the best plan is to research the pedigrees and find out whether dogs from the breeding lines in question have been successful in canine sports. You may opt to go direct to working lines, but there are many top class competitors that come from show lines, so this option should not be ruled out.

When choosing a puppy, look for a lively individual who is interested in everything that is going on. In addition, you want a puppy

Facing page: There may be a puppy who seems to say: "pick me!"

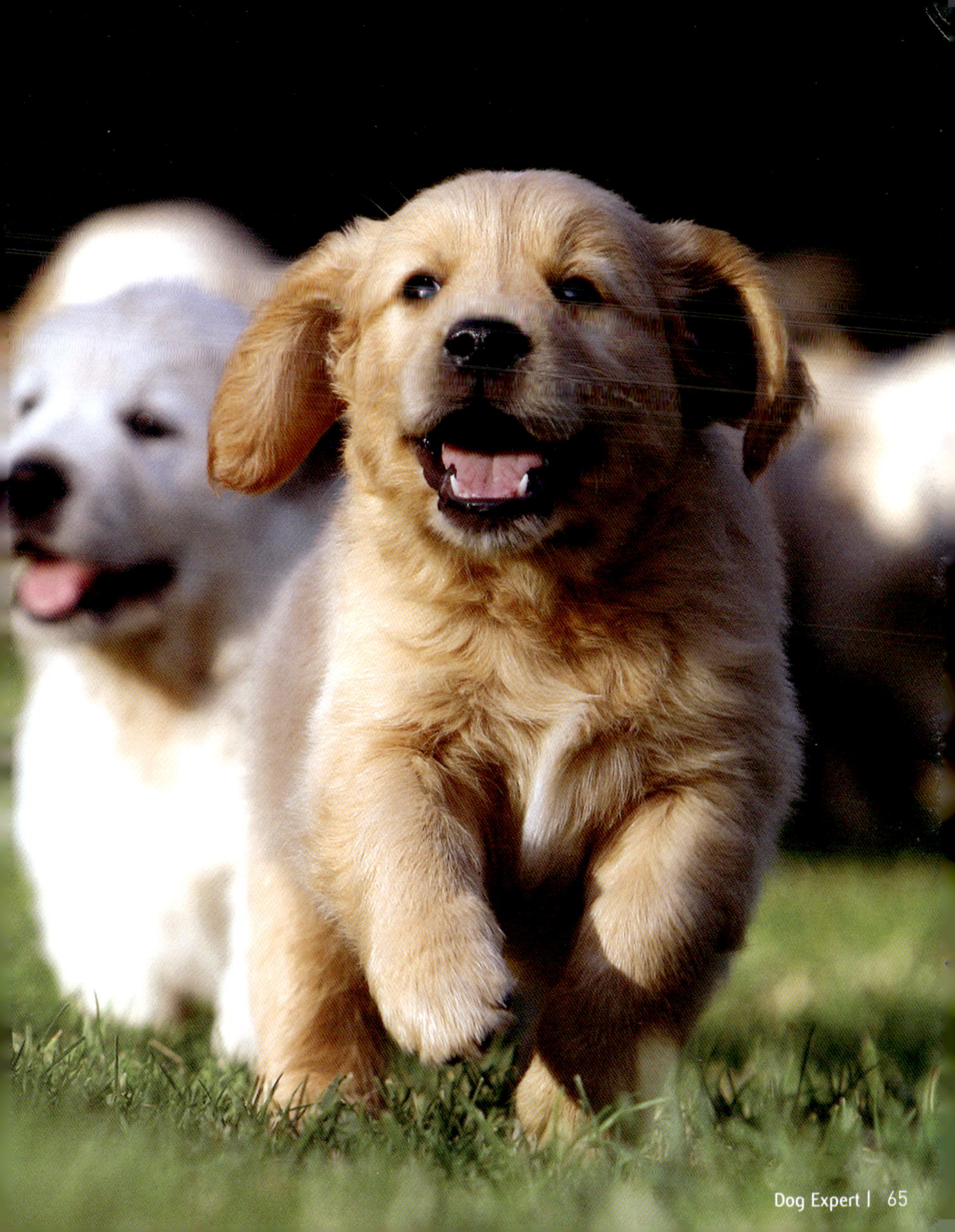

that is eager to play and who is responsive to your body language and your voice.

Show puppy

If you are buying a puppy with the hope of showing him, make this clear to the breeder. A lot of planning goes into producing a litter, and although all the puppies will have been reared with equal care, there will be one or two that have show potential.

Ideally, recruit a breed expert to inspect the puppies with you, so you have the benefit of their objective evaluation. The breeder will also be there to help as they will want to ensure that only the best of their stock is exhibited in the show ring. The best age to select a show puppy is between seven and eight weeks.

In terms of conformation, you are looking for a 'square-shaped' puppy that is not too long in the back or in the leg. The topline should be level from the shoulders to the tail. The tail should not be set on too low or too high, and it should not be 'gay' – carried over the back – which would be strongly penalised in the show ring.

One of the distinctive breed features of Golden Retrievers is the black pigment around the eyes contrasting with the beautiful golden coat, so check for dark pigment both here and on the pads. You should also check the puppy's mouth; his teeth should meet in a scissor bite (where the upper incisors closely overlap the lower) although this may be difficult to assess in such a young puppy.

It is important to bear in mind that puppies go through many phases as they are developing. A promising puppy may well go through an ugly duckling phase, and all you can do is hope that he blossoms! However, if your Goldie fails to make the grade in the show ring, he will still be an outstanding companion who will be a much-loved member of your family.

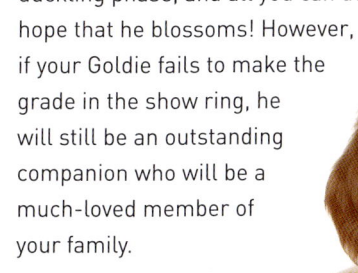

There are some essential breed points to look out for when selecting a puppy with show potential.

A Goldie-friendly home

It may seem an age before your Golden Retriever puppy is ready to leave the breeder and move to his new home. But you can fill the time by getting your home ready, and buying the equipment you will need. These preparations apply to a new puppy but, in reality, they are the means of creating an environment that is safe and secure for your Goldie throughout his life.

In the home

Nothing is safe when a puppy is about – and the Golden Retriever is certainly no exception to that rule. He likes to investigate everything he comes

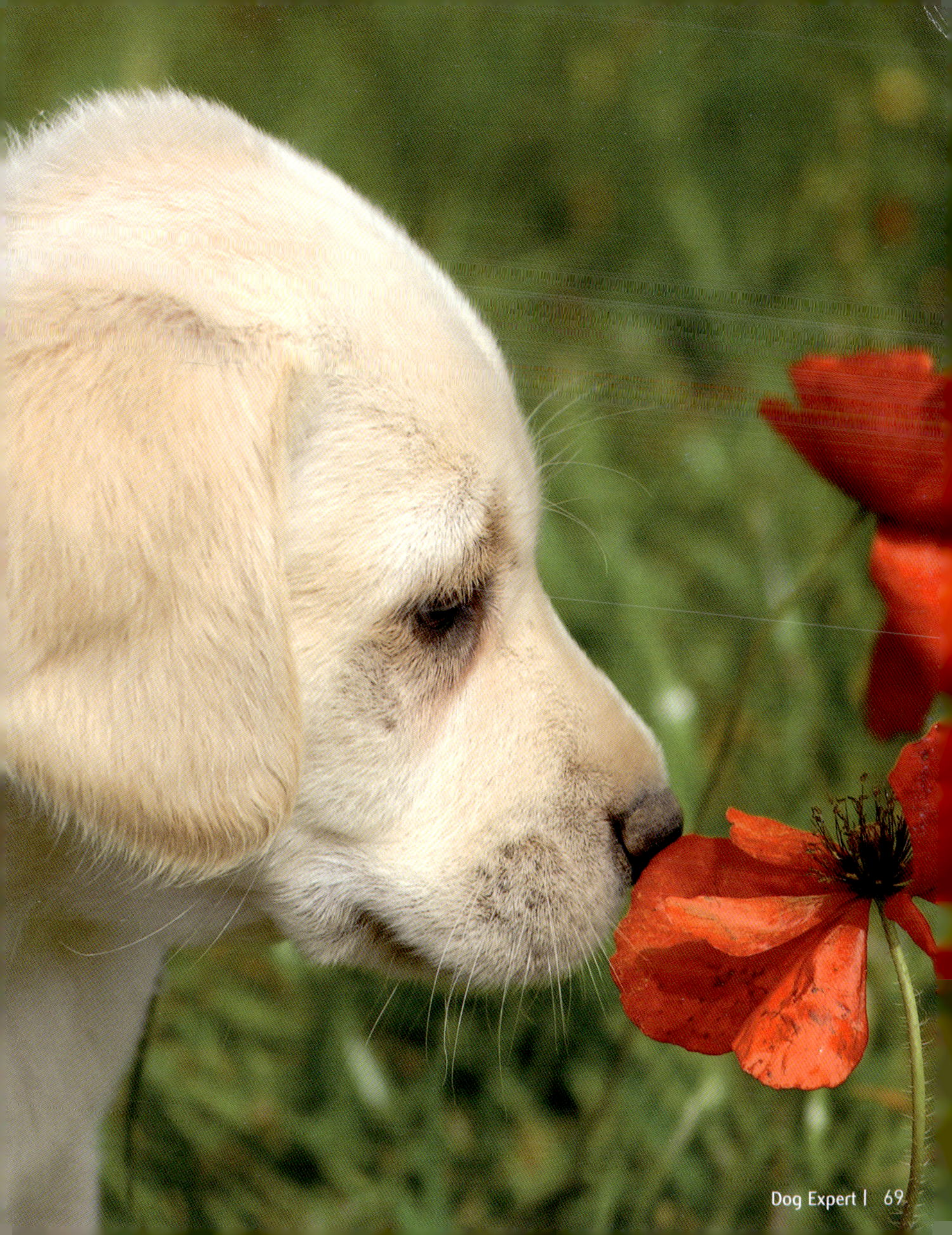

across, ideally with his mouth. Some pups like to collect trophies, others have destruction on their mind!

One thing is certain, a free-ranging Goldie puppy cannot be trusted – and this can cause big problems. Not only does it mean that your prized possessions are under threat, it could also have disastrous consequences for your puppy if he ingests something that could cause internal damage.

It is impossible to proof your entire house, so the best plan is to decide which rooms your Goldie will have access to, and make these areas puppy friendly.

Trailing electric cables are a major hazard and these will need to be secured out of reach. You will need to make sure all cupboards and storage units cannot be opened – or broken into. This applies particularly in the kitchen where you may store cleaning materials, and other substances, which could be toxic to dogs. There are a number of household plants that are poisonous, so these will need to relocated, along with breakable ornaments.

While your Golden Retriever is growing, his joints are vulnerable, so you need to reduce the risk of injury. Most owners find it is easier to make upstairs off-limits right from the start. The best way of doing this is to use a baby gate; these can also be useful if you want to limit your Goldie's freedom in any other part of the house.

In the garden

The Golden Retriever loves his family and his home, and is not much of an escape artist. However, never say never: it is important to make your garden secure so there is no chance of your Goldie making a bid for freedom.

Fencing should be a minimum of 1.5m (5ft), and gates must have secure fastenings. You also need to check the fencing to make sure it is secure and that there is no possibility of your Golden Retriever digging his way out.

Remember, nothing is safe when a Goldie is about!

If you are a keen gardener, you would be advised to protect your plants from unwanted attention by fencing them off so you have a 'people' garden and a 'dog' garden. Golden Retrievers can be enthusiastic diggers and although your Goldie may become more civilised as he matures, there are some that have a lifelong passion for digging tunnels.

You will also need to designate a toileting area. This will assist the house training process, and it will also make cleaning up easier. For information on house-training, see page 94.

House rules

Before your puppy comes home, hold a family conference to decide on the house rules. You need to decide which rooms your puppy will have access to, and establish whether he is to be allowed on the furniture or not. It is important to start as you mean to go on. You cannot invite a puppy on to the sofa for cuddles only to decide in a few months' time that this is no longer desirable.

The Golden Retriever is a biddable dog who likes to please, but he will push it if he doesn't know where his boundaries lie. If house rules are applied consistently, he will understand what is – and what is not – allowed, and he will learn to respect you and co-operate with you.

Buying equipment

There are some essential items of equipment you will need for your Golden Retriever. If you choose wisely, much of it will last for many years to come.

Indoor crate

Rearing a puppy is so much easier if you invest in an indoor crate. It provides a safe haven for your puppy at night, when you have to go out during the day, and at other times when you cannot supervise him. A puppy needs a base where he feels safe and secure, and where he can rest undisturbed. An indoor crate provides the perfect den, and many adults continue to use them throughout their lives.

Obviously you need to buy a crate that will be large enough to accommodate your Goldie when he is full-grown. He needs space to stand up, turn around, and lie at full stretch, so a crate measuring 130cm by 90cm by 60cm (45in x 24in x 36in) should be considered the minimum for an adult Golden Retriever.

You will also need to consider where you are going to locate the crate. The kitchen is usually the most suitable place as this is the hub of family life. Try to find a snug corner where the puppy can rest when he wants to, but where he can also see what is going on around him, and still be with the family.

Beds and bedding

The crate will need to be lined with bedding and the best type to buy is synthetic fleece. This is warm and cosy, and as moisture soaks through it, your puppy will not have a wet bed when he is tiny and is still unable to go through the night without relieving himself. This type of bedding is machine washable and easy to dry; buy two pieces, so you have one to use while the other piece is in the wash.

If you have purchased a crate, you may not feel the need to buy an extra bed, although your Goldie may like to have a bed in the family room so he feels part of household activities. There is an amazing array of dog-beds to chose from – duvets, bean bags, cushions, baskets, igloos, mini-four posters – so you can take your pick! However, you do need to bear in mind that a Golden Retriever can be very destructive, so you would be advised to delay making a major investment until your puppy has gone through the worst of the chewing phase.

Facing page: A crate is invaluable for the times when you cannot supervise your Goldie....

Dog Expert | 75

Collar and lead

You may think that it is not worth buying a collar for the first few weeks, but the sooner your pup gets used to it, the better (see Wearing a Collar, page 136). All you need is an adjustable, lightweight collar to start with; you will need something more substantial as your Goldie matures.

A nylon lead is suitable for early lead training, as long as the fastening is secure. You will probably need a leather lead, with a trigger fastening, when your Goldie is full grown, as nylon leads tend to chafe your hands.

ID

Your Golden Retriever needs to wear some form of ID when he is out in public places. This can be in the form of a disc, engraved with your contact details, attached to the collar. When your Goldie is full-grown, you can buy an embroidered collar with your contact details, which eliminates the danger of the disc becoming detached from the collar.

You may also wish to consider a permanent form of ID. Increasingly breeders are getting puppies micro-chipped before they go to their new homes. A micro-chip is the size of a grain of rice. It is 'injected' under the skin, usually between the shoulder blades, with a special needle. It has some tiny barbs on it, which dig into the tissue around where it lies, so it does not migrate from that spot.

Each chip has its own unique identification number which can only be read by a special scanner. That ID number is then registered on a national database with your name and details, so that if ever your dog is lost, he can be taken to any vet or rescue centre where he is scanned and then you are contacted.

If your puppy has not been micro-chipped, you can ask your vet to do it, maybe when he goes along for his vaccinations.

Bowls

Your Goldie will need two bowls; one for food, and one for fresh drinking water, which should always be readily available. A stainless steel bowl is a good choice for a food bowl as it is tough and hygienic. Plastic bowls may be chewed, and there is a danger that bacteria can collect in the small cracks that may appear.

You can opt for a second stainless steel bowl for drinking water, or you may prefer a heavier ceramic bowl which will not be knocked over so easily. Bear in mind that some Goldies think that picking up a bowl full of water is a big joke, so a heavy bowl may discourage this particular party piece!

Food

The breeder will let you know what your puppy is eating and should provide a full diet sheet to guide you through the first six months of your puppy's feeding regime – how much they are eating per meal, how many meals per day, when to increase the amounts given per meal and when to reduce the meals per day.

The breeder may provide you with some food when you collect your puppy, but it is worth making enquiries in advance about the availability of the brand that is recommended.

Grooming equipment

When your puppy first arrives, he does not need extensive coat care, but he needs to get used to being groomed. You will need the following:

- A good-quality pin brush
- Metal comb
- Guillotine nail clippers
- Toothbrush (a finger brush is easiest to use) and specially-manufactured dog toothpaste.
- Cotton-wool (cotton) pads for cleaning the eyes and ears.

Your puppy's breeder should provide you with detailed instructions on diet.

Toys

Your guiding principle when choosing a toy for a Golden Retriever is whether it is suitably robust to withstand chewing. Soft toys and plastic toys with squeakers should be avoided; opt for hard rubber toys, kongs (which can be filled with food), and tough tug toys.

You should also get into the habit of checking toys on a regular basis for signs of wear and tear. If your puppy swallows a chunk of rubber or plastic, it could cause an internal blockage. This could involve costly surgery to remove the offending item, or at worst, it could prove fatal.

Finding a vet

Before your puppy arrives home, you should register with a vet. Visit some the vets in your local area, and speak to other pet owners that you might know, to see who they recommend. It is so important to find a good vet, almost as much as finding a good doctor for yourself. You need to find someone you can build up a good rapport with and have complete faith in. Word of mouth is really the best recommendation.

When you contact a veterinary practice, find out the following:

- Does the surgery run an appointment system?

- What are the arrangements for emergency, out of hours cover?
- Do any of the vets in the practice have experience treating Golden Retrievers?
- What facilities are available at the practice?

If you are satisfied with what your find, and the staff appear to be helpful and friendly, book an appointment so your puppy can have a health check a couple of days after you collect him.

You will have fun choosing toys for your puppy – but make sure they are 100 per cent safe.

Settling in

When you first arrive home with your puppy, be careful not to overwhelm him. You and your family are hugely excited, but the puppy is in a completely strange environment with new sounds, smells and sights, which is a daunting experience, even for the boldest of pups.

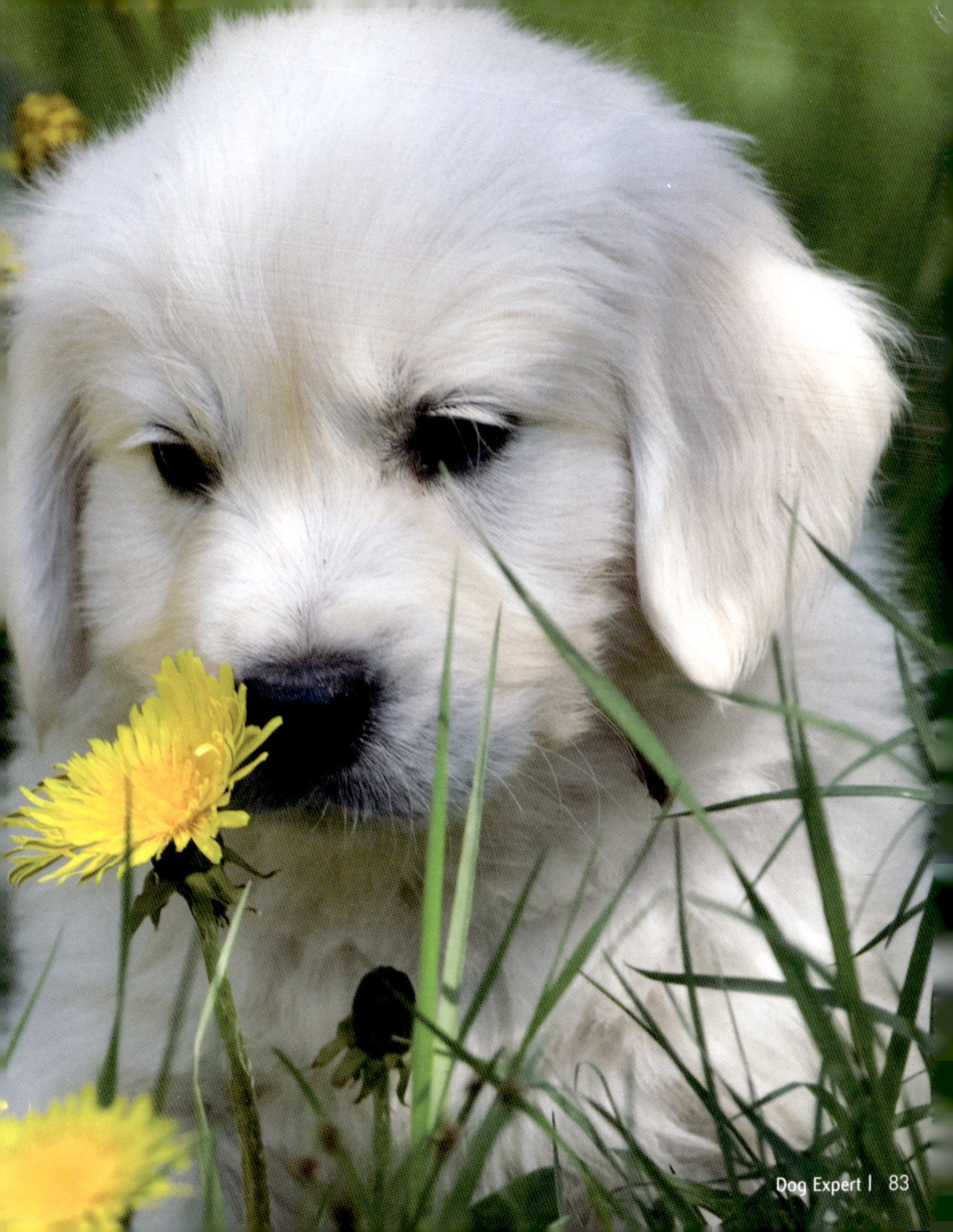

Some puppies are very confident, wanting to play straightaway and quickly making friends; others need a little longer. Keep a close check on your Golden Retriever's body language and reactions so you can proceed at a pace he is comfortable with.

First, let him explore the garden. He will probably need to relieve himself after the journey home, so take him to the allocated toileting area and when he performs give him plenty of praise.

When you take your puppy indoors, let him investigate again. Show him his crate, and encourage him to go in by throwing in a treat. Let him have a sniff, and allow him to go in and out as he wants to. Later on, when he is tired, you can put him in the crate while you stay in the room. In this way he will learn to settle and will not think he is being abandoned.

It is a good idea to feed your puppy in his crate, at least to begin with, as this helps to build up a positive association. It will not be long before your Goldie sees his crate as his own special den and will go there as a matter of choice. Some owners place a blanket over the crate, covering the back and sides, so that it is even more cosy and den-like.

Meeting the family

Resist the temptation of inviting friends and

neighbours to come and meet the new arrival; your puppy needs to focus on getting to know his new family for the first few days. Try not to swamp your Goldie with too much attention; give him a chance to explore and find his feet. There will be plenty of time for cuddles later on!

If you have children in the family, you need to keep everything as calm as possible. Your puppy may not have met children before, and even if he has, he will still find them strange and unpredictable. A puppy can become alarmed by too much noise, or he may go to the opposite extreme and become over-excited, which can lead to mouthing and nipping.

The best plan is to get the children to sit on the floor and give each of them a treat. Each child can then call the puppy, stroke him, and offer a treat. In this way the puppy is making the decisions rather than being forced into interactions he may find stressful.

If he tries to nip or mouth, make sure there is a toy at the ready, so his attention can be diverted to something he is allowed to bite. If you do this consistently, he will learn to inhibit his desire to mouth when he is interacting with people.

Right from the start, impose a rule that the children are not allowed to pick up or carry the puppy. They can cuddle him when they are sitting on the floor.

This may sound a little severe, but a wriggly puppy can be dropped in an instant, sometimes with disastrous consequences. If possible, try to make sure your Goldie is only given attention when he has all four feet on the ground. This is a breed than can be boisterous so if your pup learns that jumping up is not rewarding, it will pay dividends later on.

Involve all family members with the day-to-day care of your puppy; this will enable the bond to develop with the whole family as opposed to just one person. Encourage the children to train and reward the puppy, teaching him to follow their commands without question.

The animal family

Golden Retrievers are sociable dogs and there are rarely problems with other dogs. But if you already have a dog at home, he is likely to feel threatened by the newcomer so you need to be tactful with early interactions.

Your adult dog may be allowed to meet the puppy at the breeder's home, which is ideal as this is neutral territory as far as the older dog is concerned. But if this is not possible, allow your dog to smell the puppy's bedding (the bedding supplied by the breeder is fine) before they actually meet so he familiarises himself with the puppy's scent.

Facing page: Children can also help to take care of the family Goldie.

The garden is the best place for introducing the puppy, as there is more space and the adult will not feel as though his territory is being invaded. He will probably take a great interest in the puppy and sniff him all over. Most puppies are naturally submissive in this situation; your pup may lick the other dog's mouth or roll over on to his back. Try not to interfere as this is the natural way that dogs get to know each other.

You will only need to intervene if the older dog is too boisterous, and alarms the puppy. In this case, it is a good idea to put the adult on his lead so you have some measure of control.

It rarely takes long for an adult to accept a puppy, as he does not constitute a threat. This will be underlined if you make a big fuss of the older dog so that he has no reason to feel jealous. But no matter how well the two dogs are getting on, do not leave them alone unless one is crated.

Feline freinds

The Goldie is not a danger to cats, but unless he is taught how to behave, he can be a bit of a menace, particularly if he discovers that chasing increases the fun.

It may be easier if the cat is confined in a carrier for the first couple of meetings so your puppy has a chance to make his acquaintance in a controlled situation. Keep calling your puppy to you and rewarding him so that he does not focus too intently on the cat. You can then graduate to holding your puppy while the cat is free, again rewarding him with a treat every time he responds to you and looks away from the cat. When you allow your puppy to go free, make sure the cat has an easy escape route, just in case he tries to chase.

This is an on-going process but, all the time your Goldie is learning that he is rewarded for ignoring the cat. In time, the novelty will wear off and the pair will live in harmony. Indeed, there is a many a Golden Retriever that has gone on to form a close friendship with the family cat.

Feeding

The breeder will generally provide enough food for the first few days so the puppy does not have to cope with a change in diet – and possible digestive upset – along with all the stress of moving home.

Some puppies eat up their food from the first meal onwards, others are more concerned by their new surroundings and are too distracted to eat. Do not worry unduly if your puppy seems disinterested in his food for the first day or so.

Give him 10 minutes to eat what he wants and then remove the leftovers and start afresh at the next meal. Obviously if you have any concerns about your puppy in the first few days, seek advice from your vet.

Golden Retrievers are not normally possessive over their food, but it is advisable to guard against this tendency from day one. If you have children, you need to establish a rule that no one is to go near the dog when he is feeding. This is sound commonsense, and removes all risk of problems arising, no matter how unintentional they may be.

At the same time, you can educate your Goldie so that he does not become stressed if people are around when he is eating. You can do this by giving him half his ration, and then dropping food around his bowl. This will stop him guarding his bowl and, at the same time, he will see your presence in a positive light. You can also call him away from the bowl and reward him with food – maybe something extra special – which he can take from your hand.

Start doing this as soon as your puppy arrives in his new home, and continue working on it throughout his life. Remember, food is a top priority for a dog; he will respect you as the provider and, if you interact with him as described, he will trust you and will not feel threatened.

The first night

Your puppy will have spent the first weeks of his life either with his mother or curled up with his siblings. He is then taken from everything he knows as familiar, lavished with attention by his new family – and then comes bed time when he is left all alone. It is little wonder that he feels abandoned.

The best plan is to establish a night-time routine, and then stick to it so that your puppy knows what is expected of him. Take your puppy out into the garden to relieve himself, and then settle him in his crate. Some people leave a low light on for the puppy at night for the first week, others have tried a radio as company or a ticking clock. A covered hot-water bottle, filled with warm water, can also be a comfort. Like people, puppies are all individuals and what works for one, does not necessarily work for another, so it is a matter of trial and error.

Be very positive when you leave your puppy on his own; do not linger, or keep returning; this will make the situation more difficult. It is inevitable that he will protest to begin with, but if you stick to your routine, he will accept that he gets left at night – but you always return in the morning.

Rescued dogs

Settling an older, rescued dog in the home is very similar to a puppy in as much as you will need to make the same preparations regarding his homecoming. As with a puppy, an older dog will need you to be consistent, so start as you mean to go on.

There is often an initial honeymoon period when you bring a rescued dog home, where he will be on his best behaviour for the first few weeks. It is after these first couple of weeks that the true nature of the dog will show, so be prepared for subtle changes in his behaviour. It may be advisable to register with a reputable training club, so you can seek advice on any training or behavioural issues at an early stage.

Above all, remember that a rescued dog ceases to be a rescued dog the moment he enters his forever home and should be treated normally like any other family dog.

A rescued dog needs your patience and understanding as he settles in a new home.

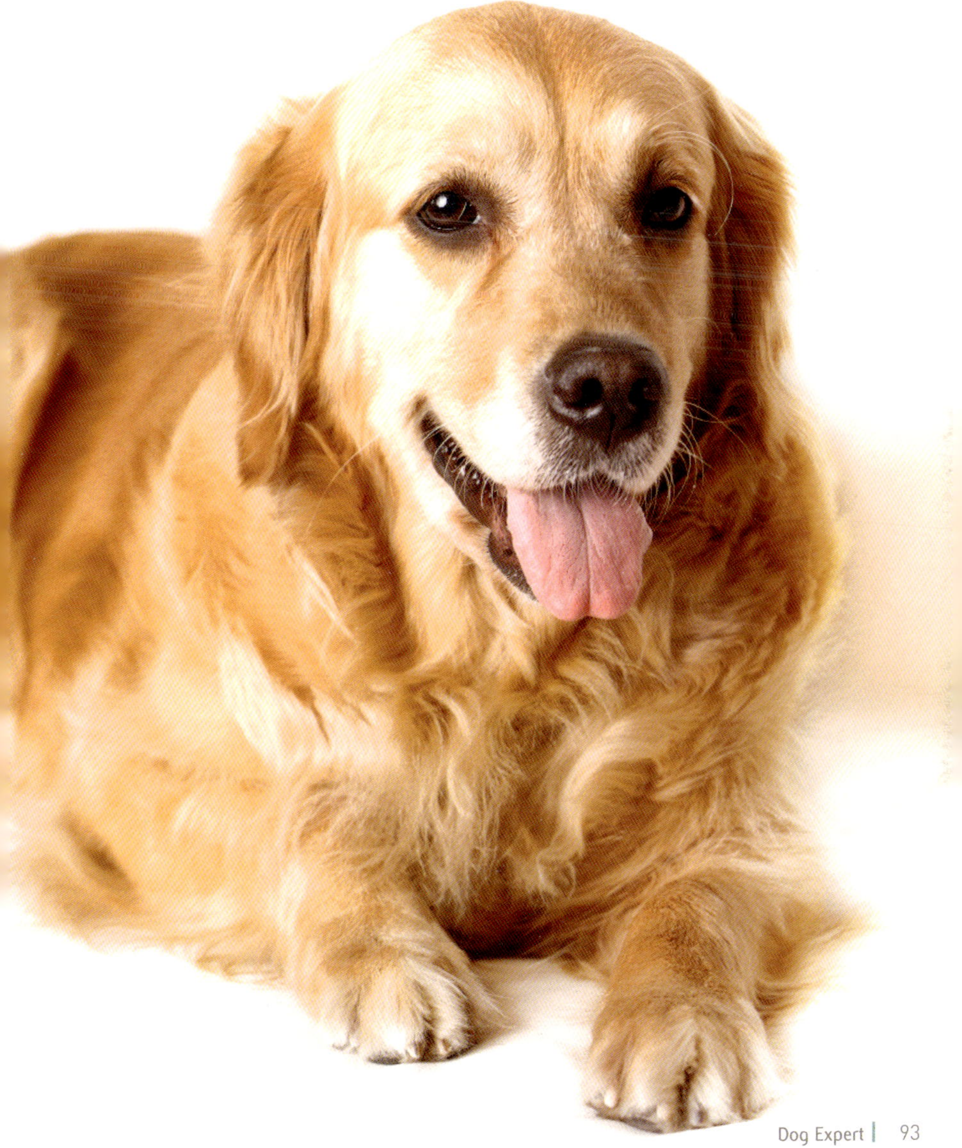

House training

This is the aspect of training that puppy owners dread – but it doesn't have to be an ordeal if you put in the time and effort in the first few weeks.

Dog Expert | 95

The key to successful house training is vigilance and consistency. If you establish a routine, and you stick to it, your puppy will understand what is required. Equally, you must be there to supervise him at all times – except when he is safely tucked up in his crate. It is when a puppy is left to wander from room to room that accidents are most likely to happen.

As discussed earlier, you will have allocated a toileting area in your garden when preparing for your puppy's homecoming. You need to take your puppy to this area every time he needs to relieve himself so he builds up an association and knows why you have brought him out to the garden.

Establish a routine and make sure you take your puppy out at the following times:

- First thing in the morning
- After mealtimes
- On waking from a sleep
- Following a play session
- Last thing at night.

A puppy should be taken out to relieve himself every two hours as an absolute minimum. If you can manage an hourly trip out, so much the better. The more often your puppy gets it 'right', the quicker he will learn to be clean in the house. It helps if you use a verbal cue, such as "Busy", when your pup is performing and, in time, this will trigger the desired response.

Do not be tempted to put your puppy out on the doorstep in the hope that he will toilet on his own. Most pups simply sit there, waiting to get back inside the house! No matter how bad the weather is, accompany your puppy and give him lots of praise when he performs correctly.

Do not rush back inside as soon as he has finished; your puppy might start to delay in the hope of prolonging his time outside with you. Praise him, have a quick game – and then you can both return indoors.

When accidents happen

No matter how vigilant you are, there are bound to be accidents. If you witness the accident, take your puppy outside immediately, and give him lots of praise if he finishes his business out there.

If you are not there when he has an accident, do not scold him when you discover what has happened. He will not remember what he has done and will not understand why you are cross with him. Simply clean it up and resolve to be more vigilant next time.

Choosing a diet

There are so many different types of dog food on sale – all claiming to be the best – so how do you know what is likely to suit your Golden Retriever? This is an active dog that needs a well-balanced diet suited to his individual requirements.

When choosing a diet, there are basically three categories to choose from:

Complete

This is probably the most popular diet as it is easy to feed and is specially formulated with all the nutrients your dog needs. This means that you should not add any supplements, or you may upset the nutritional balance.

Most complete diets come in different life stages –puppy, adult maintenance and senior – so this

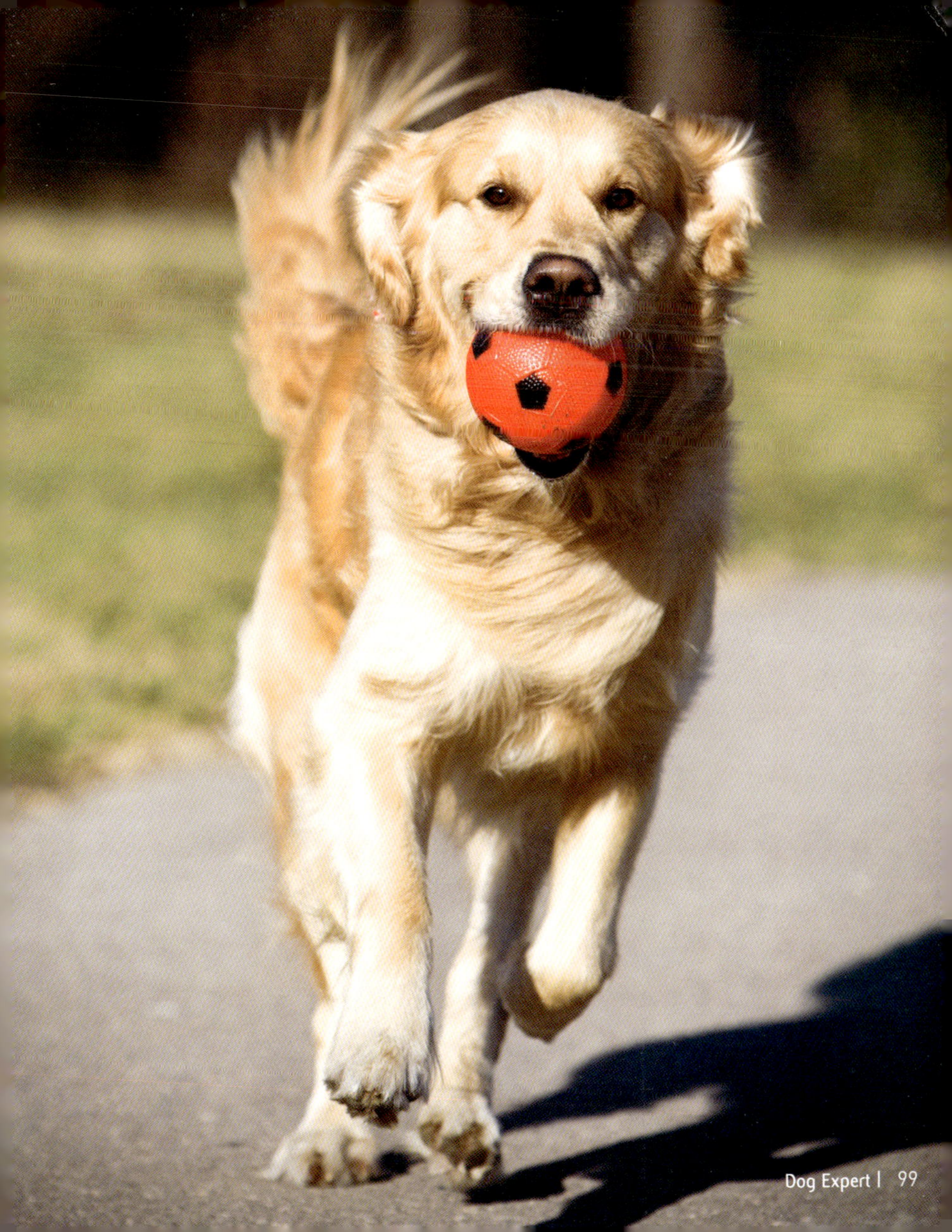

means that your Goldie is getting what he needs when he is growing, during adulthood, and as he becomes older. You can even get prescription diets for dogs with particular health issues.

Generally, an adult maintenance diet should contain 21 to 24 per cent protein and 10 to 14 per cent fat. Protein levels should be higher in puppy diets, and reduced in veteran diets. If your Goldie becomes over-excitable for no obvious reason, it is worth checking the levels of protein in his food and possibly reducing the calorie intake. It has been proved that protein overload can have a significant effect on a dog's behaviour.

There are many different brands to choose from so it is advisable to seek advice from your puppy's breeder who will have lengthy experience of feeding Golden Retrievers.

Canned/pouches

This type of food is usually fed with hard biscuit, and most Golden Retrievers find it very appetising. However, the ingredients – and the nutritional value – do vary significantly between the different brands, so you will need to check the label. This type of food often has a high moisture content, so you need to be sure your Goldie is getting all the nutrition he needs.

Homemade

There are some owners who like to prepare meals especially for their dogs and it is probably much appreciated. The danger is that although the food is tasty, and your Golden Retriever may enjoy the variety, you cannot be sure that it has the correct nutritional balance.

If this is a route you want to go down, you will need to find out the exact ratio of fats, carbohydrates, proteins, minerals and vitamins that are needed, which is quite an undertaking.

The Barf (Biologically Appropriate Raw Food) diet is another, more natural approach to feeding. Dogs are fed a diet mimicking what they would have eaten in the wild, consisting of raw meat, bone, muscle, fat, and vegetable matter. Golden Retrievers appear to do well on this diet so it is certainly worth considering. There are now a number of companies that specialise in producing the Barf diet in frozen form, which makes preparation a lot easier, particularly for the squeamish!

Feeding regime

When your puppy arrives in his new home he will need four meals, evenly spaced throughout the day. You may decide to keep to the diet recommended by your puppy's breeder, and if your pup is thriving there is no need to change. However, if your puppy is not doing well on the food, or you have problems with supply, you will need to make a change.

When switching diets, do so on a gradual basis, changing over from one food to the next, a little at a time, and spreading the transition over a week to 10 days. This will avoid the risk of digestive upset.

When your puppy is around 12 weeks, you can cut out one of his meals; he may well have started to leave some of his food indicating he is ready to do this. By six months, he can move on to two meals a day – a regime that will suit him for the rest of his life.

Bones and chews

Puppies love to chew, and many adults also enjoy gnawing on a bone. Bones should always be hard and uncooked; rib bones and poultry bones must be avoided as they can splinter and cause major problems. Dental chews, and some of the manufactured rawhide chews are safe, but they should only be given under supervision.

Facing page: A Goldie needs a well balanced diet which matches his energy output.

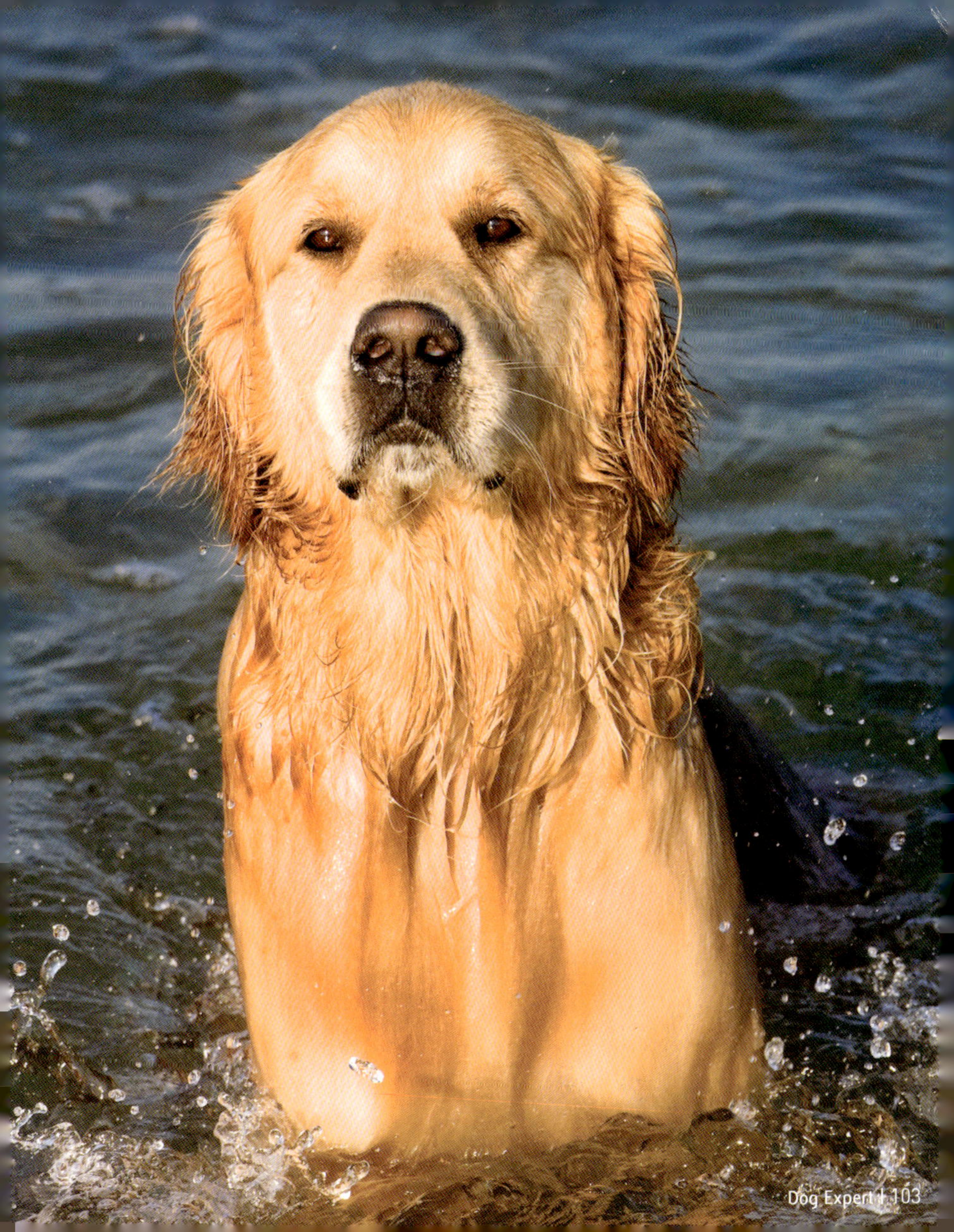

Ideal weight

In order to help to keep your Golden Retriever in good health it is necessary to monitor his weight. A Goldie has a way of looking at you with his melting, dark brown eyes, and persuading you that he is starving to death! Before you know it, your Goldie starts to pile on the pounds, and becomes vulnerable to serious health problems.

The major issue is feeding too much food in relation to the amount of energy your dog is expending. This is easily done if you follow feeding guidelines on packet foods, rather than monitoring your dog's individual weight and lifestyle.

The Golden Retriever has a close-fitting coat so there is no disguising his figure! Make sure that when you look at your dog from above he has a definite 'waist'. You should be able to feel his ribs, but not see them.

In order to keep a close check on your Goldie's weight, get into the habit of visiting your veterinary surgery on a monthly basis so that you can weigh him. Keep a record of his weight so you can make adjustments if necessary. Remember, it is no kindness to over-feed a Golden Retriever; obesity has a significant effect on your dog's quality of life and his life expectancy.

If you are concerned that your Goldie is putting on too much weight, consult your vet who will help you to plan a suitable diet.

It is your responsibility as an owner to keep your Goldie at the correct weight.

Caring for your Goldie

The Golden Retriever is a breed without exaggeration and, as a result, he is relatively easy to care for. But, like all animals, a Goldie has his own special needs which you must take on board.

Puppy grooming

When your Golden Retriever puppy first arrives in his new home at around eight weeks of age, he will have a fluffy coat, which does not really need grooming. However, this is going to change as the adult coat comes through, and daily grooming will be required.

It is therefore important to accustom your puppy to a routine of grooming, so that he learns to relax and enjoy the attention. All dogs need to accept handling without fear or resentment so that you can attend to their care needs. Trips to the vet will also be far less stressful if your Goldie will tolerate being examined without making a fuss.

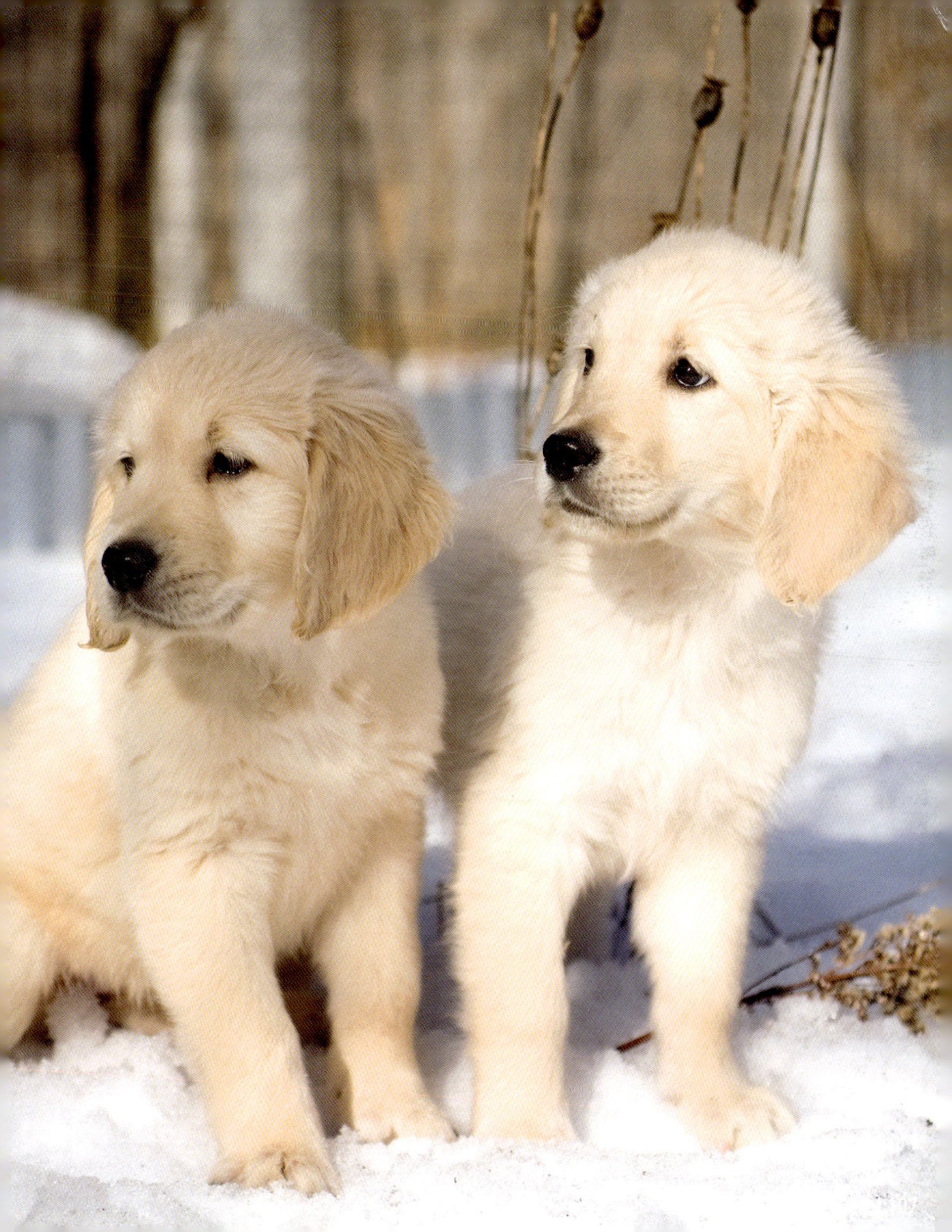

Start by handling your puppy all over, stroking him from his head to his tail. Lift up each paw in turn, and reward him with a treat when he co-operates. Then roll him over on to his back and tickle his tummy; this is a very vulnerable position for a dog to adopt, so do not force the issue. Be firm but gentle, and give your puppy lots of praise when he does as you ask.

When your Goldie is happy to be handled in this way, you can introduce a soft brush and spend a few minutes grooming the coat, and then reward him. Take your time and be patient; your Goldie will gradually learn to accept the attention and will relax while you groom him.

Adult grooming

An adult Golden Retriever may have a wavy coat or a flat coat; both types have a dense undercoat. However, it is the feathering that increases the workload. Ideally, you should set aside a few minutes every day to groom your Goldie and then once a week give him a more thorough going over.

Start by working through the coat with a wire pin brush – one with flexible pins is best. Brush in the direction the coat lies, using firm strokes. The process of grooming helps to distribute the natural oils in the coat which bring out its sheen, and it also aids circulations.

A wire pin brush is ideal for working through the coat.

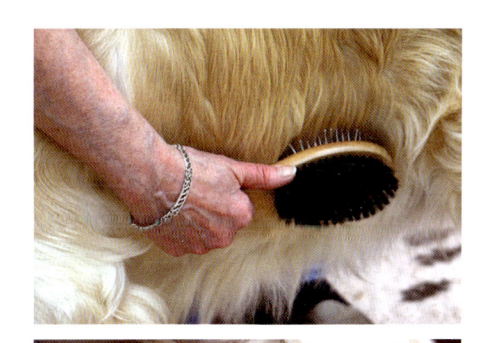

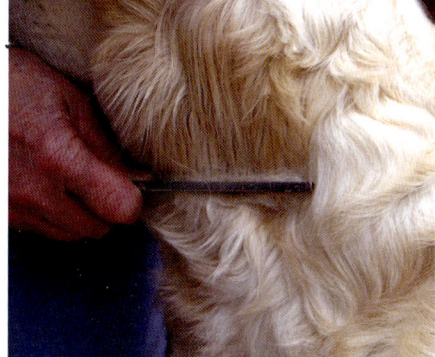

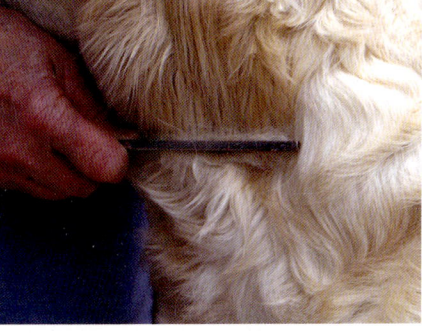

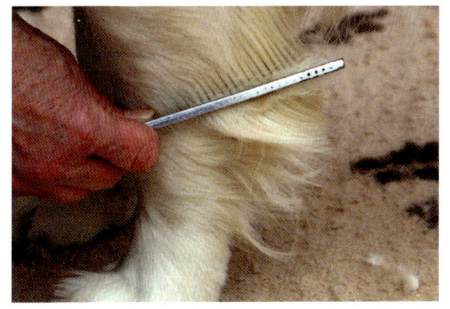

Next use a metal comb.

Pay particular attention to the feathering.

Dog Expert | 109

You will need a metal comb to work through the feathering. This can be quite a painstaking job; the long hair can mat and tangle very easily, particularly in the areas behind the ears, around the elbows and in the groin area. However, the more often you groom, the less work is needed, so make sure you do not leave it too long between grooming sessions.

If you want your Golden Retriever to look really smart, you can finish by going over his coat with a hound glove. As the name indicates, this grooming tool is worn as a glove. One side is covered with shorter metal pins, which are useful for brushing through the coat, and the other side, covered in material, is used for 'buffing up' and bringing out the shine.

Bathing is only needed on an occasional basis – usually when your Goldie has decided to roll in something smelly, which is a Golden Retriever speciality! For this reason, it is a good idea to bath your dog before he needs it, so you can both get used to the procedure.

Trimming

Golden Retrievers that are exhibited in the show ring are trimmed to enhance their appearance. This is not necessary for pet dogs, but it is important to keep a check on your Goldie's feet. If the hair grows

Show dogs need to be trimmed.

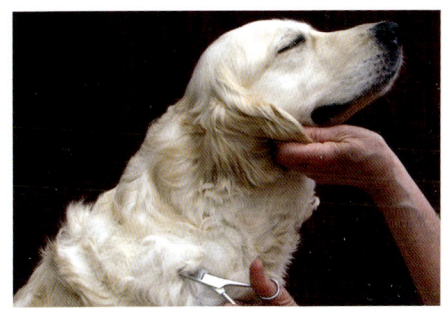

Trimming the hair around the feet is also beneficial for pet dogs.

It is important to get rid of the hair that grows between the pads.

between the pads, it can become very uncomfortable so this will need to be kept in trim using straight-edged scissors. It is also worth trimming the hair around the feet so they look neat and tidy, and this will reduce the amount of dirt and debris your dog brings into the house.

Show dogs should still look natural, but their contours are improved with a little judicious trimming. Show exhibitors trim the following areas:

- The front of the neck, using thinning scissors, to make the neck look long and elegant.

- Along the tail, making the feathering fall in a natural curve which makes the dog look more balanced.

- Behind the ears so that the ears lie flat.

- Around the feet to give a neat, cat-like appearance.

Routine care

In addition to grooming, you will need to carry out some routine care.

Eyes

The eyes should always be bright with no trace of soreness or discharge. Occasionally, first thing in the morning, you may notice a small amount of discharge. This is nothing to worry about – just wipe it away using a damp cotton pad, making sure you use a separate pad for each eye.

However, if your Golden Retriever continually has discharge or watery eyes, or his eyes look dull, you should consult your vet.

Ears

The ears should be clean and free from odour. You can buy specially-manufactured ear wipes, or you can use a cotton pad and an ear wash to clean them if necessary.

Dampen the pad with ear wash and gently wipe round the inside surface of the dog's ear. Try to reach the nooks and crannies, but do not poke deeper into the ear canal as you could cause damage. Allow your dog to shake off any excess moisture; this will help prevent infection.

Teeth

Teeth cleaning should be seen as an essential part of your care regime. Look for warning signs of gum disease such as bad breath, red and swollen gums, a yellow-brown crust of tartar around the teeth, and pain or bleeding when you touch the gums or mouth. You should also watch for discoloured, fractured, or missing teeth. Any bumps or masses within the mouth should also be checked your vet.

Regular teeth cleaning means that you will prevent problems arising, or, at the very least, you will spot trouble at an early stage and will be able to take the appropriate action. Bear in mind that if tartar is allowed to accumulate, there may be no option but to get it removed by a vet, which involves a general anaesthetic.

When your Golden Retriever is still a puppy, accustom him to teeth cleaning so it becomes a matter of routine. Dog toothpaste comes in a variety of meaty flavours, which your Goldie will like, so you can start by putting some toothpaste on your finger and gently rubbing his teeth. You can then progress to using a finger brush or a toothbrush, whichever you find most convenient.

Remember to reward your Goldie when he co-operates and then he will positively look forward to his teeth-cleaning sessions.

Nails

Nail trimming is a task which worries many owners – and many dogs – but, again, if you start early on, your Golden Retriever will get used to the procedure. Hopefully, the breeder will have started the process by trimming the puppies' nails when they are just

Clean the ears with specially formulated ear-wipes or with some damp cotton-wool (cotton).

Regular teeth cleaning should be considered essential.

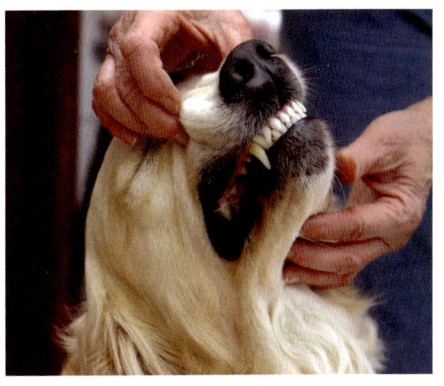

Nail trimming needs to be carried out on a routine basis.

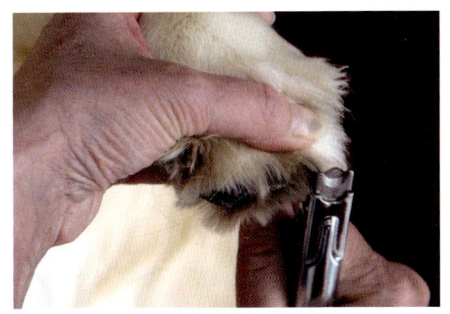

a few weeks' old to stop them scratching their mother's underside when they are feeding.

If your dog has white nails, you will be able to see the quick (the vein that runs through the nail), which you must avoid at all costs. If you cut the quick it will bleed profusely and cause considerable discomfort. Obviously, the task is much harder in dark nails as you cannot see the quick. The best policy is to trim little and often so the nails don't grow too long, and you do not risk cutting too much and catching the quick.

If you are worried about trimming your Golden Retriever's nails, go to your vet so you can see it done properly. If you are still concerned, you can always use the services of a professional groomer.

Exercise

The Golden Retriever was bred to be a versatile retriever, working on land and in water. As such, he is built to be on the go for long periods, often in cold, wet conditions. So, the result is we have a hardy, energetic dog who needs regular, physical exercise. Although the majority of Golden Retrievers are now companions rather than working gundogs, this essential requirement should not be neglected.

To begin with, you have the opposite problem. A young Golden Retriever puppy should not be over-exercised as it puts too much strain on vulnerable joint, which can lead to lasting damage. A puppy will get as much exercise as he needs playing in the garden. Once he has completed his vaccinations, he will need to be socialised, which will involve lead walking exercise.

Always err on the side of caution, and return home before your puppy is tired. Walking on hard surfaces, such as pavements, combined with the mental stimulation of taking in new experiences, is exhausting, and could lead to your puppy having a negative experience if you overdo it.

As your puppy grows and develops, you can gradually step up his exercise – both lead walking and free running. An adult Golden Retriever needs a minimum of two 30 minute exercise sessions a day– and if you can manage more, so much the better!

As a working gundog, the Golden Retriever is expected to retrieve from water as well as on land. Goldies are excellent swimmers, and many have an uncanny knack of finding water, even in near desert conditions! Swimming is a very beneficial form of exercise, bul try to get to the water before your Goldie and check that it is safe, with no strong currents, and with easy access in and out.

When you are planning exercise sessions, remember that mental stimulation is as important as physical exercise. Try to give your Golden Retriever the opportunity to use his brain by playing retrieve games with him, or getting him to use his nose by sniffing out treats or a favourite toy.

Dog Expert | 119

Golden oldies

The Golden Retriever has a good life expectancy. Many will reach their early teens, and some their mid-teens.

The older Goldie will sleep more, and he may be reluctant to go for longer walks. He may show signs of stiffness when he gets up from his bed, but these generally ease when he starts moving. Some older Golden Retrievers may have impaired vision, and some may become a little deaf, but as long as their senses do not deteriorate dramatically, this is something older dogs learn to live with.

If you treat your older Goldie with consideration, he will enjoy his later years and suffer the minimum of discomfort. It is advisable to switch him over to a senior diet, which is more suited to his needs, and you may need to adjust the quantity, as he will not be burning up the calories as he did when he was younger and more energetic. Make sure his sleeping quarters are warm and free from draughts, and, if he gets wet and muddy on a walk (more than likely with a Goldie!), make sure you dry him thoroughly.

Most important of all, be guided by your dog. He will have good days when he feels up to going for a walk, and other days when he would prefer to potter in the garden. If you have a younger dog at home, this may well stimulate your Goldie to take more of an interest in what is going on, but make sure he is not pestered as he needs to rest undisturbed when he is tired.

Letting go

Inevitably there comes a time when your Golden Retriever is not enjoying a good quality of life, and you need to make the painful decision to let him go. We would all wish that our dogs died, painlessly, in their sleep but, unfortunately, this is rarely the case.

However, we can allow our dogs to die with dignity, and to suffer as a little as possible, and this should be our way of saying thank you for the wonderful companionship they have given us.

When you feel the time is drawing close, talk to your vet, who will be able to make an objective assessment of your Golden Retriever's condition and will help you to make the right decision.

This is the hardest thing you will ever have to do as a dog owner, and it is only natural to grieve for your beloved Goldie. But eventually, you will be able to look back on the happy memories of times spent together, and this will bring much comfort. You may, in time, feel that your life is not complete without a Golden Retriever, and you will feel ready to welcome a new puppy into your home.

Social skills

To live in the modern world, without fears and anxieties, your Golden Retriever needs to receive an education in social skills so that he learns to cope calmly and confidently in a wide variety of situations. The Goldie is generally a confident dog, with no hang-ups, so if you spend time socialising him in his first 12 months, he will be set for life.

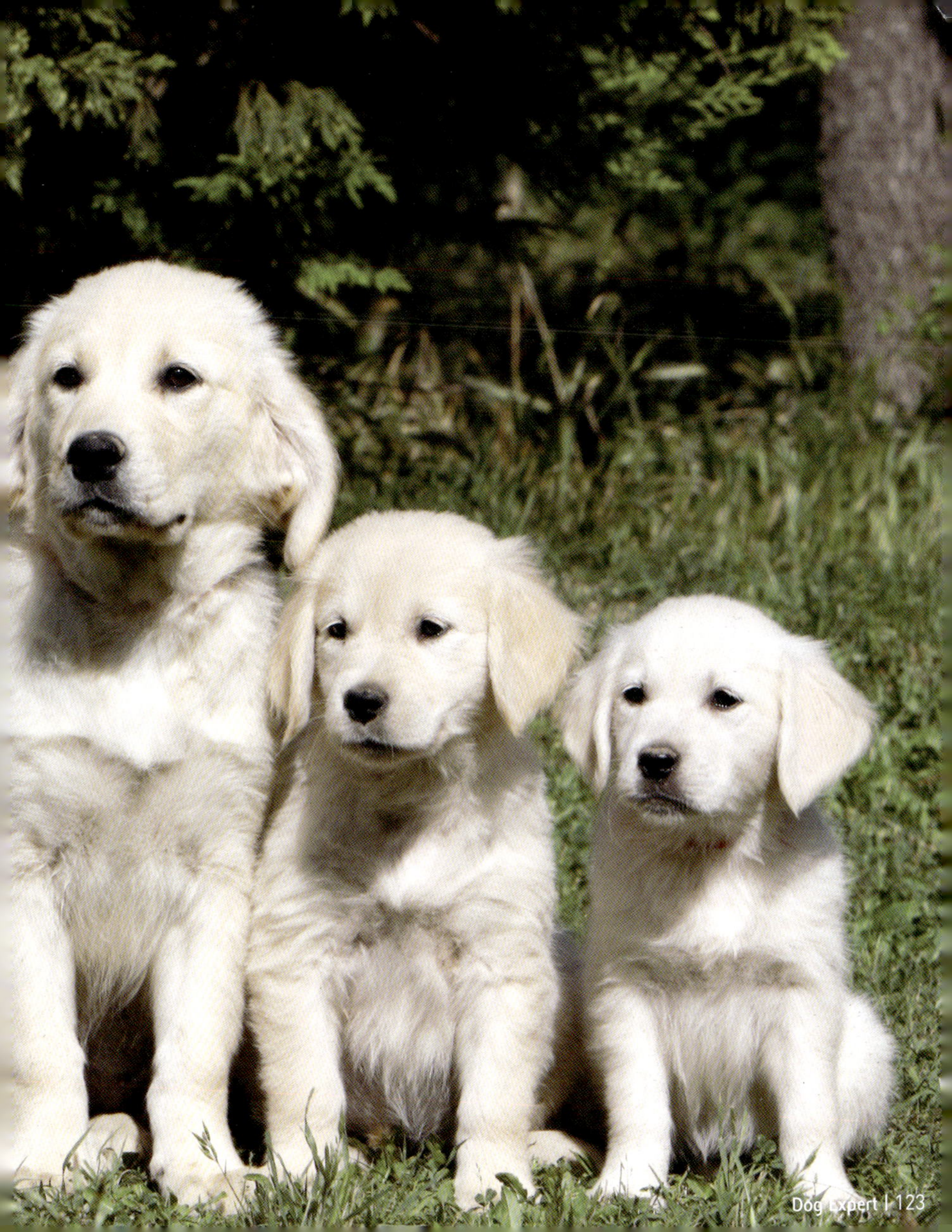

Early learning

The breeder will have begun a programme of socialisation by getting the puppies used to all the sights and sounds of a busy household. You need to continue this when your pup arrives in his new home, making sure he is not worried by household equipment, such the vacuum cleaner or the washing machine, and that he gets used to unexpected noises from the radio and television.

As already highlighted, it is important that you handle your puppy on a regular basis so he will accept grooming and other routine care, and will not be worried if he has to be examined by the vet.

To begin with, your puppy needs to get used to all the members of his new family, but then you should give him the opportunity to meet visitors to your house. Golden Retrievers are naturally friendly and outgoing, but sometimes they can be a little boisterous. A friendly greeting is one thing; being knocked for six is quite another! It is therefore important that your Goldie learns appropriate greeting behaviour right from the start.

Bear in mind that most Golden Retrievers think that bringing a gift is an essential part of greeting, so it may pay to have a few appropriate items near at hand...

Puppies have so much to learn in their first few months.

When visitors arrive at your home, adopt the following procedure:

- Make sure your Golden Retriever is on the lead so you are in control.
- When you answer the door, make sure you have treats at the ready.
- Ask your Goldie to "Sit" before opening the door, and reward him with a treat.
- When you open the door, make sure he remains in the Sit, correcting him (and rewarding again) if necessary.
- The next step is to ask the visitor to give your Goldie a treat, but makes sure he remains in the Sit.

Dog Expert | 125

This process is quite long-winded, so the best plan is to practise with friends who are used to dogs, so your Goldie understands what is required.

If you do not have children, make sure your puppy has the chance to meet and play with other people's children, so he learns that humans come in small sizes, too.

The outside world

When your puppy has completed his vaccinations, he is ready to venture into the outside world. In most cases a Golden Retriever puppy will take a lively interest in anything new and will relish the opportunity to broaden his horizons. However, there is a lot for a youngster to take on board, so do not swamp him with too many new experiences.

You also need to be aware that the Golden Retriever has a stubborn streak, and he may decide that a sit down strike is called for, even though there is no apparent reason for it. If this happens, do not be confrontational – and never lose your patience. This is simply a phase you have to work through.

Arm yourself with treats and adopt a firm, no-nonsense attitude, as if you are unaware your Goldie is failing to co-operate. The moment he moves forward, give him lots of praise, and perhaps run a few steps, so that he gets caught up in the fun. For more advice, see Lead Training, page 136.

The best plan is to start socialising your puppy in a quiet area with light traffic, and only progress to a busier place when he is ready. There is so much to see and hear – people (maybe carrying bags or umbrellas), pushchairs, bicycles, cars, lorries, machinery – so give your puppy a chance to take it all in.

If he does appear worried, do not fall into the trap of sympathising with him, or worse still, picking him up. This will only teach your pup that he had a good reason to be worried and, with luck, you will 'rescue' him if he feels scared.

Instead, give him a little space so he does not have to confront whatever he is frightened of, and distract him with a few treats. Then encourage him to walk past, using an encouraging tone of voice, never forcing him by yanking on the lead. Reward him for any forward movement, and your puppy will soon learn that he can trust you, and there is nothing to fear.

Your pup also needs to continue his education in canine manners, started by his mother and by his littermates, as he needs to be able to greet all dogs calmly, giving the signals that say he is friendly and offers no threat. If you have a friend who has a dog of sound temperament, this is an ideal beginning. As your puppy gets older and more established, you can widen his circle of canine acquaintances.

Training classes

A training class will give your Golden Retriever the opportunity to work alongside other dogs in a controlled situation, and he will also learn to focus on you in a different, distracting environment. Both these lessons will be vital as your Goldie matures.

However, the training class needs to be of the highest calibre, or you risk doing more harm than good. Before you go along with your puppy, attend a class as an observer to make sure you are happy with what goes on.

Find out the following:

- How much training experience do the instructors have?
- Are the classes divided into appropriate age categories?

Progress at a speed your puppy is comfortable with.

- Do the instructors have experience training gundogs?
- Do they use positive, reward-based training methods?

If the training class is well run, it is certainly worth attending. Both you and your Goldie will learn useful training exercises; it will increase his social skills, and you will have the chance to talk to lots of like-minded dog enthusiasts.

Training guidelines

The Golden Retriever is a biddable dog and he likes to please his human family. He is highly intelligent and picks up new exercises quickly, so your job is to provide a positive learning environment.

You will be keen to get started, but in your rush to get training underway, do not neglect the fundamentals which could make the difference between success and failure.

When you start training, try to observe the following guidelines:

- Choose an area that is free from distractions so your puppy will focus on you. You can progress to a more challenging environment as your pup progresses.

- Do not train your puppy just after he has eaten

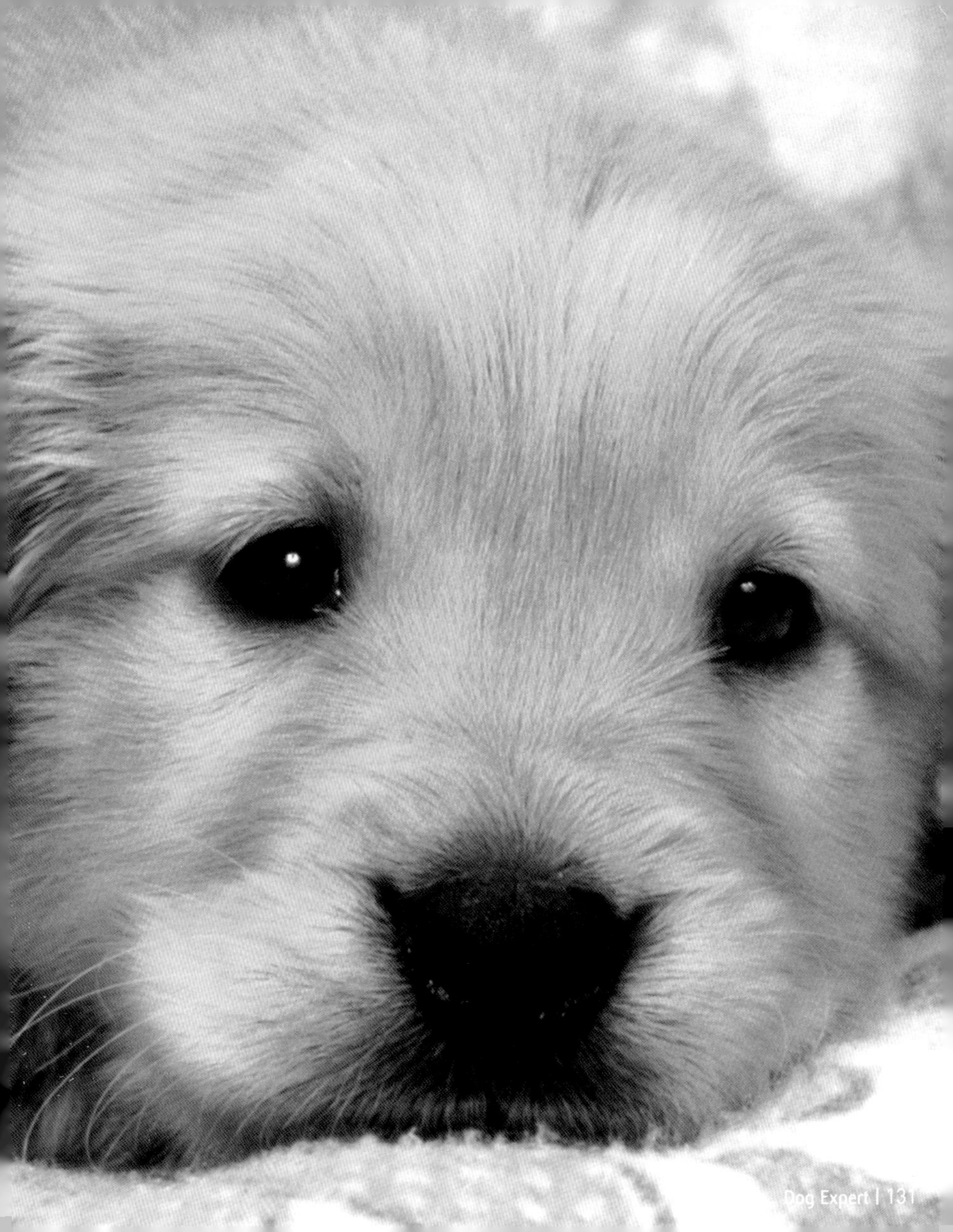

or when you have returned from exercise. He will either be too full, or too tired, to concentrate.

- Do not train if you are in a bad mood, or if you are short of time – these sessions always end in disaster!

- Make sure you have a reward your Golden Retriever values – tasty treats, such as cheese or cooked liver, or an extra special toy which you reserve for training sessions.

- If you are using treats, make sure they are bite-size, otherwise you will lose momentum when your pup stops to chew on his treat.

- Keep your verbal cues simple, and always use the same one for each exercise. For example, when you ask your puppy to go into the Down position, the cue is "Down", not "Lie Down", Get Down", or anything else... Remember your Goldie does not speak English; he associates the sound of the word with the action.

- If your Goldie is finding an exercise difficult, break it down into small steps so it is easier to understand.

- Do not make your training sessions boring and repetitious; your Goldie will quickly lose interest and he may cease to co-operate.

- Do not train for too long, particularly with a young puppy, who has a very short attention span, and always end training sessions on a positive note. This does not necessarily mean getting an exercise right. If your pup is tired and making mistakes, ask him to do a simple trick or exercise so you have the opportunity to praise and reward him. You may well find that he benefits from having a break and will make better progress next time you try.

- Above all, make training fun so you and your Goldie enjoy spending quality time together.

Find a reward that your Goldie values.

First lessons

Like all puppies, a young Golden Retriever will soak up new experiences like a sponge, so training should start from the time your pup arrives in his new home. It is so much easier to teach good habits rather than trying to correct your puppy when he has established an undesirable pattern of behaviour.

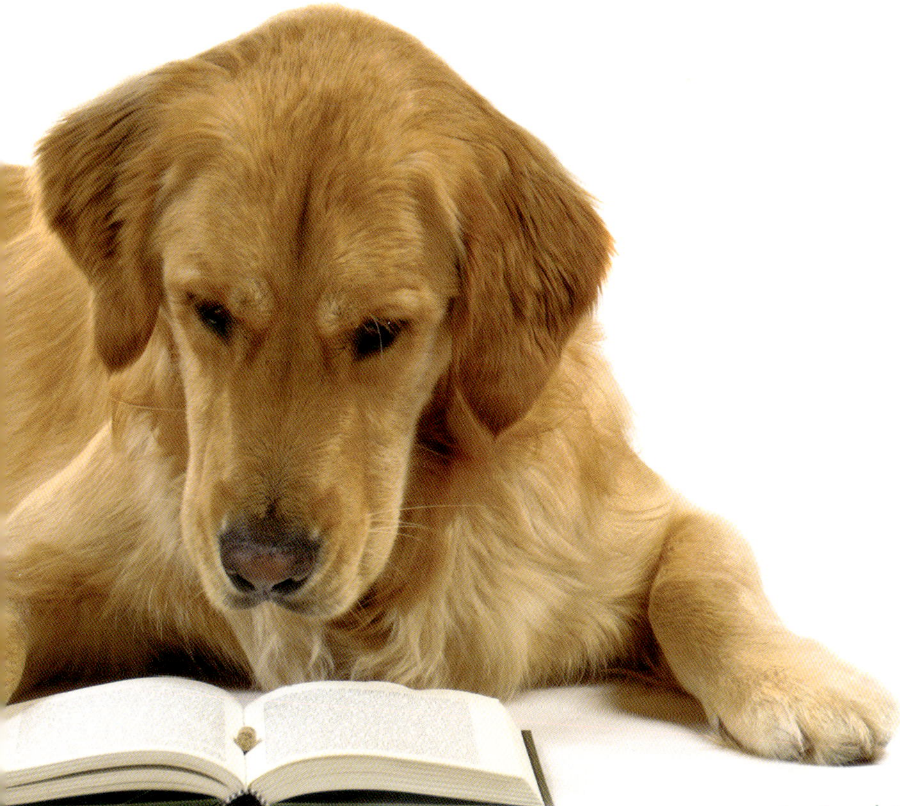

Wearing a collar

You may, or may not, want your Goldie to wear a collar all the time. But when he goes out in public places he will need to be on a lead, and so he should be used to the feel of a collar around his neck. The best plan is to accustom your pup to wearing a soft collar for a few minutes at a time until he gets used to it.

Fit the collar so that you can get at least two fingers between the collar and his neck. Then have a game to distract his attention. This will work for a few moments; then he will stop, put his back leg up behind his neck and scratch away at the peculiar itchy thing round his neck, which feels so odd.

Bend down, rotate the collar, pat him on the head and distract him by playing with a toy or giving him a treat. Once he has worn the collar for a few minutes each day, he will soon ignore it and become used to it.

Remember, never leave the collar on the puppy when he is unsupervised, especially outside in the garden or when he is in his crate, as it is could get snagged, causing serious injury.

Walking on the lead

This sounds easy, but it is an exercise that frustrates many owners – and Golden Retriever puppies have something of a reputation for stubbornness in this department! At one moment your Goldie is walking by your side like a real pro, the next he has jammed on the brakes and is refusing to move.

It can be very frustrating, often exacerbated by onlookers giving helpful advice... However, this is just a Golden Retriever 'thing' and if you have patience (and a sense of humour) your puppy will soon get over it.

Once your puppy is used to the collar, take him outside into your secure garden where there are no distractions.

Attach the lead and, to begin with, allow him to wander with the lead trailing, making sure it does not become snagged up. Then pick up the lead and follow the pup where he wants to go; he needs to get used to the sensation of being attached to you.

The next stage is to get your Goldie to follow you, and for this you will need some tasty treats. It is a good idea to reserve some really high-value treats, such as cooked liver, specifically for lead training so your Goldie has the best possible incentive to co-operate.

Show your puppy that you have a treat in your hand, and then encourage him to follow you. Walk a few paces, and if he is walking with you, stop and reward him. If he puts on the brakes, simply change direction and lure him with the treat.

Next, introduce some changes of direction so your puppy is walking confidently alongside you. At this stage, introduce a verbal cue "Heel" when your puppy is in the correct position.

You can then graduate to walking your puppy outside the home – as long as he has completed his vaccination programme – starting in quiet areas and building up to busier environments.

Training strategy

When you start taking your Goldie out and about on the lead you may experience problems. He may suddenly decide to go on strike, not because he is being naughty, but because he is overwhelmed by the new sights and sounds he is encountering.

All he needs is a little time to process what he is seeing and hearing, so give him a few moments to look and learn. Then encourage him to go forwards, attracting his attention with a treat, and rewarding him the instant he co-operates.

You may find that outings have a bit of a stop/start quality to begin with, but if you don't make a big deal of it, your pup will find it is more interesting to keep walking than to be at a standstill. Remember, keep training lighthearted and reward at frequent intervals.

Be prepared to spend a considerable amount of time to establish good lead walking as it will have far-reaching effects. If your Golden Retriever gets into bad habits when he is on the lead, you will soon start excluding him from expeditions where you know this will be a problem. However, if your Goldie is trained to walk calmly beside you, on a loose lead, he will become your constant companion, and will be a pleasure to own.

Patience, repetition and lots of rewards are needed when lead training.

Come when called

The Golden Retriever is an energetic dog who loves the opportunity to free run and to investigate all the fascinating smells he comes across. You can only allow your dog this type of freedom if he has a reliable recall.

The Golden Retriever is a people orientated dog and, in most cases, he will not stray too far away and will be happy to come back to you. However, there will be times when he finds a scent, a muddy puddle, or an open stretch of water, and you find he has suddenly developed selective hearing. You need to develop a strategy which means that your Goldie always thinks that returning to you is the most rewarding option.

The key to successful recall training is to start early. Hopefully, the breeder will have laid the foundations simply by calling the puppies to "Come" at mealtimes, or when moving from one place to another.

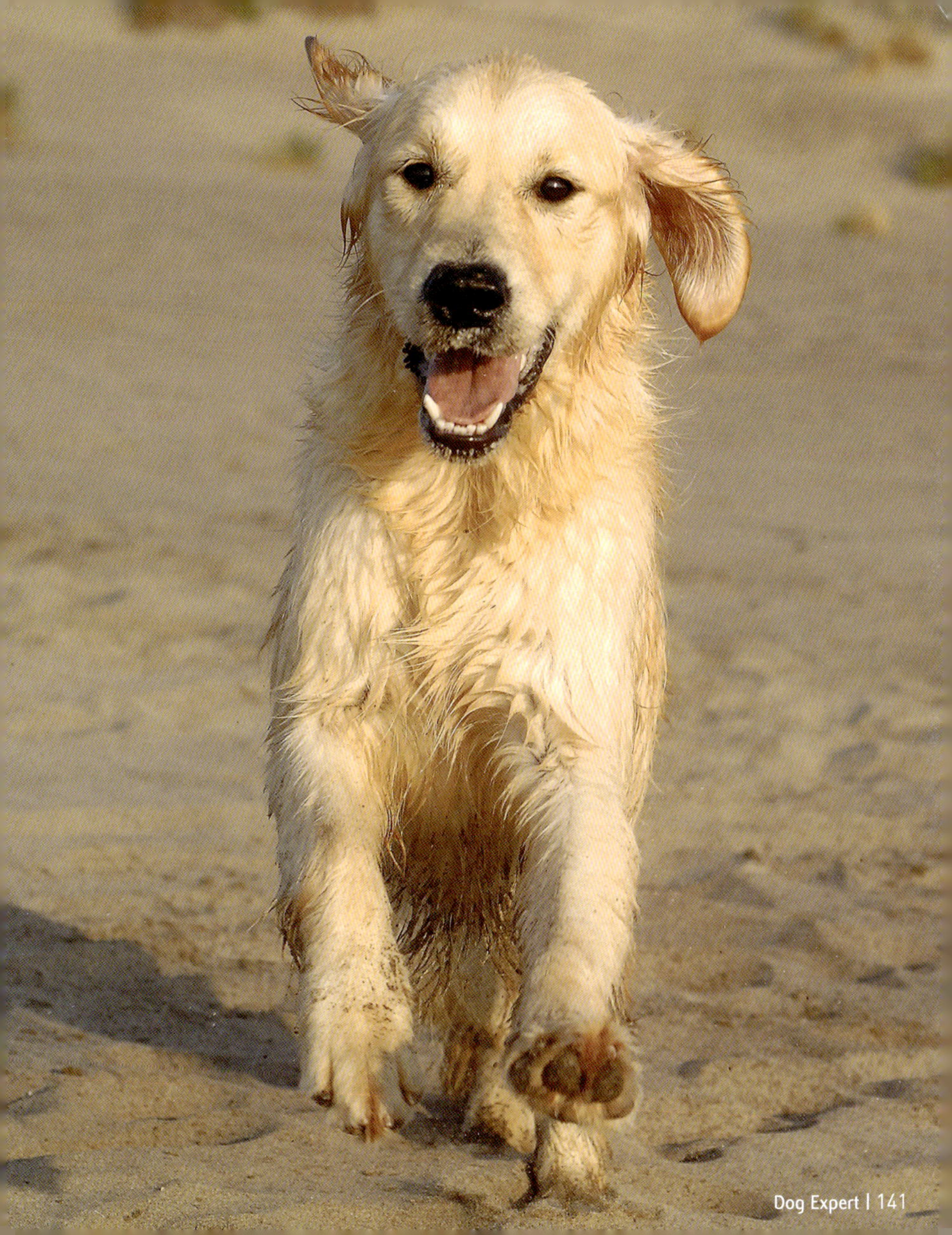

You can build on this when your puppy arrives in his new home, calling him to "Come" when he is in a confined space, such as the kitchen. This is a good place to build up a positive association with the verbal cue – particularly if you ask your puppy to "Come" to get his dinner!

The next stage is to transfer the lesson to the garden. Arm yourself with some treats, and wait until your puppy is distracted. Then call him, using a higher-pitched, excited tone of voice. At this stage, a puppy wants to be with you, so capitalise on this and keep practicing the verbal cue, rewarding your puppy with a treat and lots of praise when he comes to you.

Now you are ready to introduce distractions. Try calling him when someone else is in the garden, or wait a few minutes until he is investigating a really interesting scent. When he responds, make a really big fuss of him and give him some extra treats so he knows it is worth his while to come to you. If your puppy responds, immediately reward him with a treat.

If he is slow to come, run away a few steps and then call again, making yourself sound really exciting. Jump up and down, open your arms wide to welcome him; it doesn't matter how silly you look, he needs to see you as the most fun person in the world.

When you have a reliable recall in the garden, you can venture into the outside world. Do not be too ambitious to begin with; try a recall in a quiet place with the minimum of distractions, so you can be assured of success

Do not make the mistake of only asking your dog to come at the end of his allotted exercise period. What is the incentive in coming back to you if all you do is clip on his lead, marking the end of his free time? Instead, call your dog at random times, giving him a treat and a stroke, and then letting him go free again. In this way, coming to you is always rewarding, and does not signal the end of his free run.

Make sure your Goldie is always rewarded for coming back to you.

Stationary exercises

The Sit and Down are easy to teach, and mastering these exercises will be rewarding for both you and your Golden Retriever.

Sit

The best method is to lure your Goldie into position, and for this you can use a treat, a toy, or his food bowl.

- Hold the reward (a treat or food bowl) above his head. As he looks up, he will lower his hindquarters and go into a sit.

- Practise this a few times and, when your puppy understands what you are asking, introduce the verbal cue, "Sit".

- When your Goldie understands the exercise, he will respond to the verbal cue alone, and you

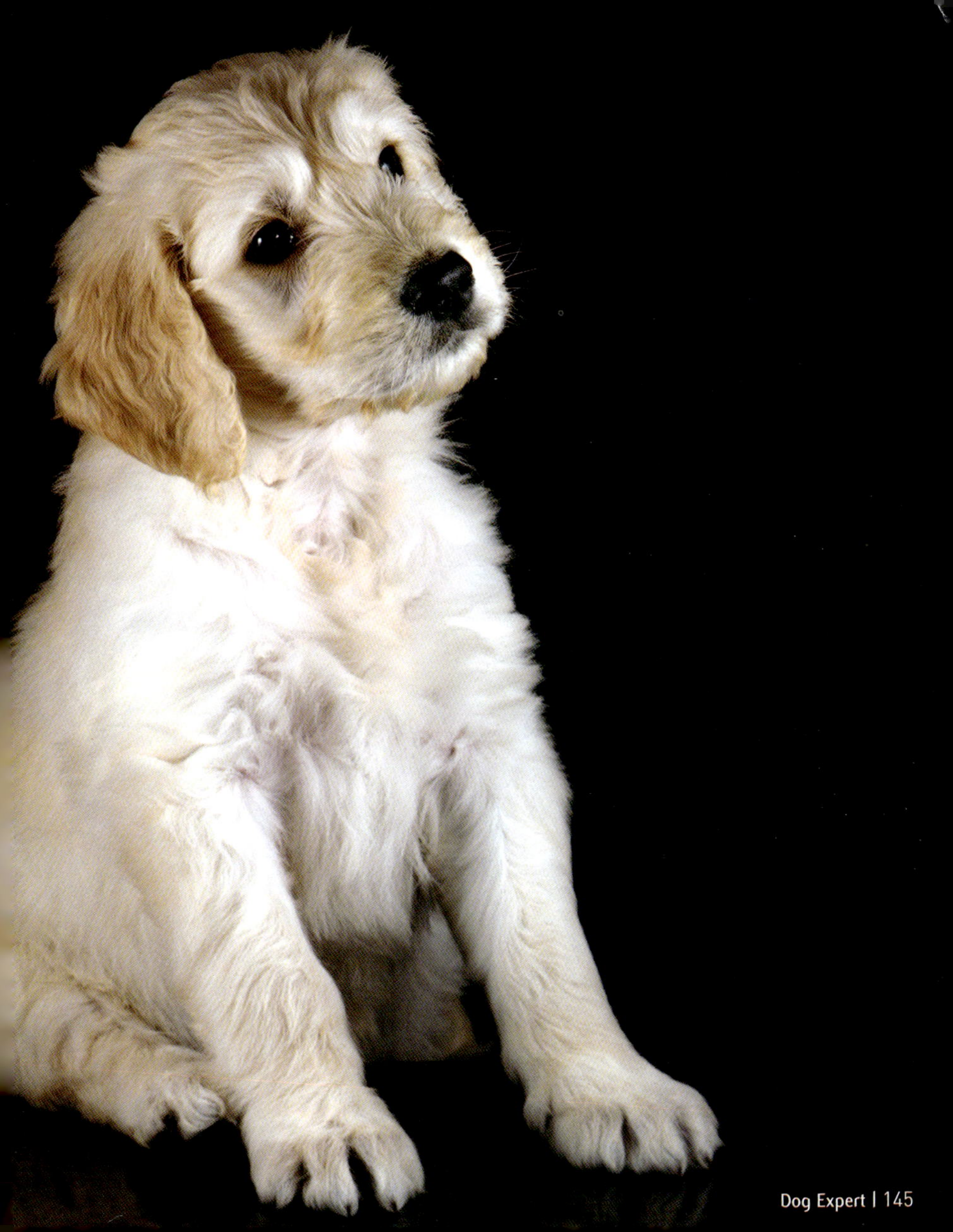

will not need to reward him every time he sits. However, it is a good idea to give him a treat on a random basis when he co-operates to keep him guessing!

Down

This is an important lesson, and can be a lifesaver if an emergency arises and you need to bring your Golden Retriever to an instant halt.

You can start with your dog in a Sit or a Stand for this exercise. Stand or kneel in front of him and show him you have a treat in your hand. Hold the treat just in front of his nose and slowly lower it towards the ground, between his front legs.

As your Goldie follows the treat he will go down on his front legs and, in a few moments, his hindquarters will follow. Close your hand over the treat so he doesn't cheat and get the treat before he is in the correct position. As soon as he is in the Down, give him the treat and lots of praise.

Keep practising, and when your Goldie understands what you want, introduce the verbal cue "Down".

Facing page: Gradually increase the length of time your Goldie will stay in the Down.

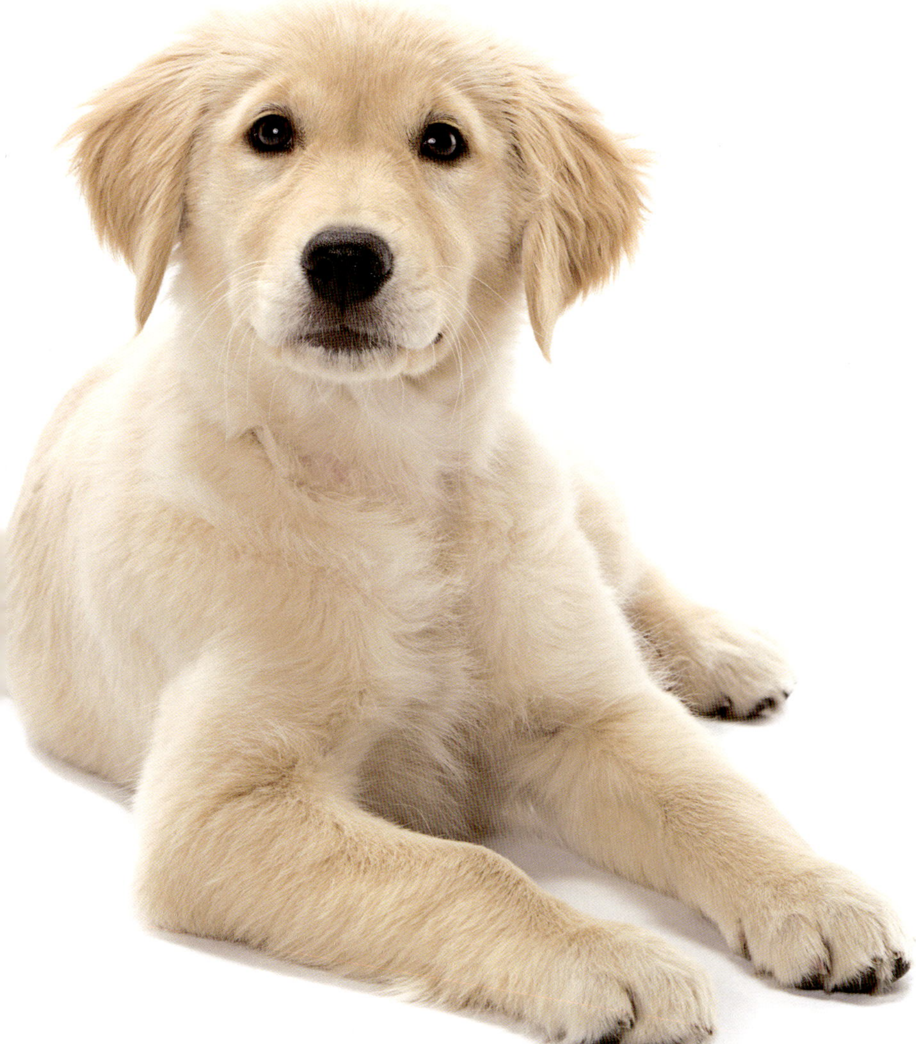

Control exercises

These exercises are not the most exciting, particularly for a young dog who wants to be on the go. However, they are useful in a variety of situations, and can go a long way towards keeping your Goldie safe. These exercises also teach your Golden Retriever that you are someone to be respected, and, if he co-operates, he is always rewarded for making the right decision.

Wait

This exercise teaches your Goldie to "Wait" in position until you give the next command; it differs from the Stay exercise where he must stay where you have left him for a more prolonged period. The most useful application of "Wait" is when you are getting your dog out of the car and you need

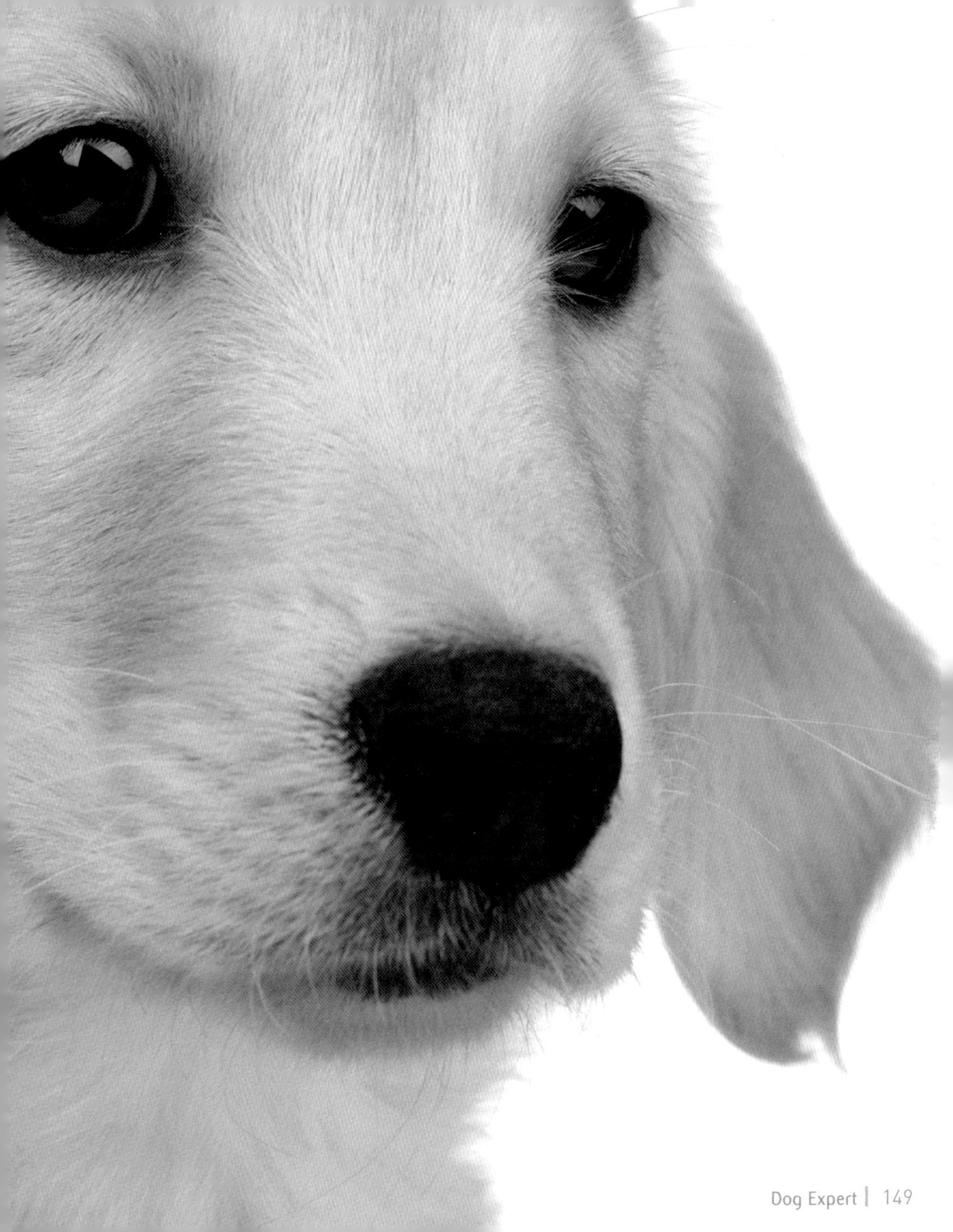

him to stay in position until you clip on his lead.

Start with your puppy on the lead to give you a greater chance of success. Ask him to "Sit", and stand in front him. Step back one pace, holding your hand, palm flat, facing him. Wait a second and then come back to stand in front of him again. You can then reward him and release him with a word, such as "OK".

Practise this a few times, waiting a little longer before you reward him, and then introduce the verbal cue "Wait".

You can reinforce the lesson by using it in different situations, such as asking your Goldie to "Wait" before you put down his food bowl.

Stay

You need to differentiate this exercise from the Wait by using a different hand signal and a different verbal cue.

Start with your Golden Retriever in the Down as he most likely to be secure in this position. Stand by his side and then step forwards, with your hand held back, palm facing the dog.

Step back, release him, and then reward him. Practice until your Goldie understands the exercise and then introduce the verbal cue "Stay".

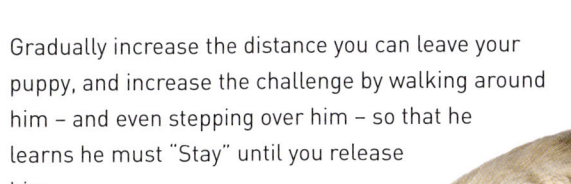

Gradually increase the distance you can leave your puppy, and increase the challenge by walking around him – and even stepping over him – so that he learns he must "Stay" until you release him.

Leave

A response to this verbal cue means that your Golden Retriever will learn to give up a toy on request, and it follows that he will give up anything when he is asked, which is very useful if he has hold of a forbidden object.

This is particularly helpful in the case of Goldies who will pick up anything they come across when they are excited.

Your Goldie must learn to give up a toy on request.

You can also use the cue to "Leave" if you catch your Goldie red-handed raiding the bin, or stealing food from a kitchen surface.

- The "Leave" command can be taught quite easily when you are first playing with your puppy. As you gently take a toy from his mouth, introduce the verbal cue, "Leave", and then praise him.

- If he is reluctant, swap the toy for another toy or a treat. This will usually do the trick.

- Do not try to pull the toy from his mouth if he refuses to give it up, as they will only make him keener to hang on to it. Let the toy go 'dead' in your hand, and then swap it for a new, exciting toy, so this becomes the better option.

- Remember to make a big fuss of your Golden Retriever when he co-operates. If he is rewarded with verbal praise, plus a tasty treat or a game with a toy, he will learn that "Leave" is always a good option.

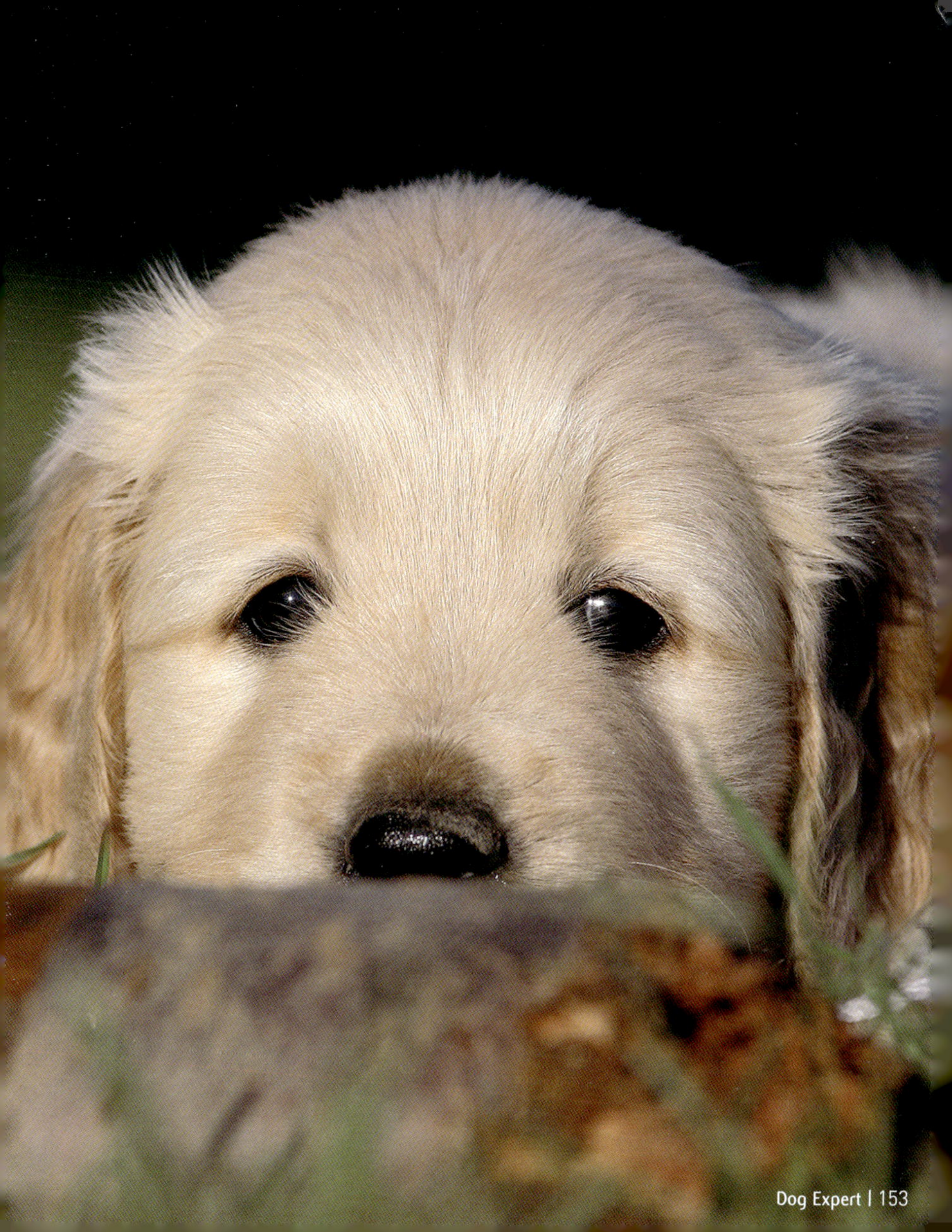

Opportunities for Goldies

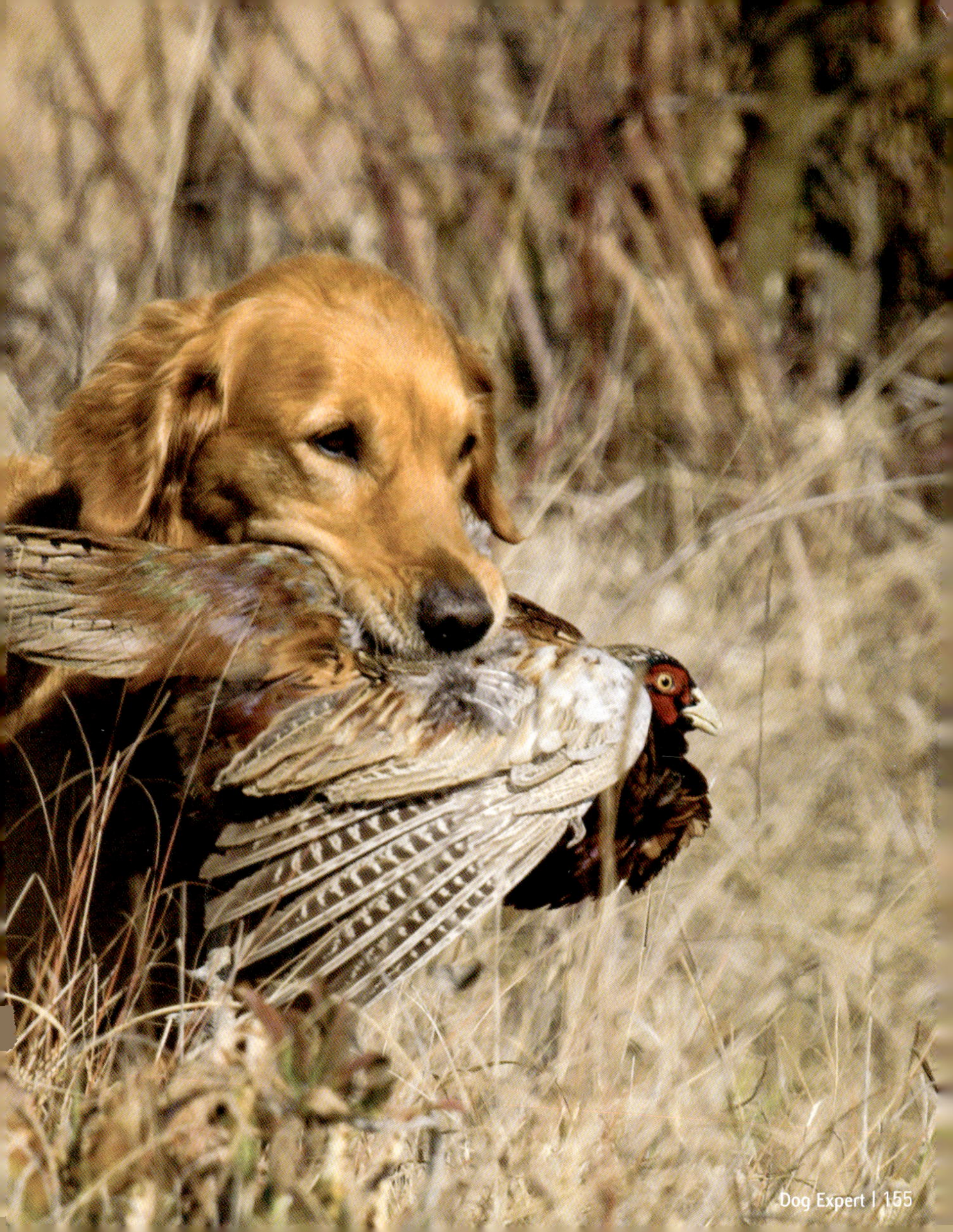

The Golden Retriever thrives on mental stimulation and he will be delighted if you want to advance his training and get involved in one of the canine sports. He is a natural all-rounder and has made his mark in many of the disciplines.

Good Citizen Scheme

The Kennel Club Good Citizen Scheme was introduced to promote responsible dog ownership, and to teach dogs basic good manners. In the US there is one test; in the UK there are four award levels: Puppy Foundation, Bronze, Silver and Gold.

Exercises within the scheme include:

- Walking on a lead
- Road walking
- Control at door/gate
- Food manners
- Recall
- Stay
- Send to bed
- Emergency stop

Obedience

If your Golden Retriever has mastered basic obedience, you may want to get involved in Competitive Obedience. The exercises include heelwork at varying paces with dog and handler following a pattern decided by the judge, stays, recalls, retrieves, sendaways, scent discrimination and distance control. The exercises get progressively harder as you move up the classes.

A Golden Retriever will readily learn the exercises that are used in obedience competitions, and a number have done well at the highest level, competing on a par with Border Collies and German Shepherd Dogs. However, it is a discipline that calls for a very high degree of precision and accuracy which does not suit all dogs, or all handlers.

Rally O

If you do not want to get involved in the rigours of Competitive Obedience, you may find that a sport called Rally O is more to your liking.

This is loosely based on Obedience, and also has a few exercises borrowed from agility when you get to the highest levels. Handler and dog must complete a course, in the designated order, which has a variety of different exercises numbering between 12 and 20.

The course is timed and the team must complete within the time limit that is set, but there are no bonus marks for speed.

The great advantage of Rally O is that it is very relaxed, and anyone can compete; indeed, it has proved very popular for handlers with disabilities as they are able to work their dogs to a high standard and compete on equal terms with other competitors.

Cannicross

This is a relatively new sport and it is tailor-made for fit owners who have dogs with high exercise requirements. Basically, it involves cross-country running attached to your dog. You will need some specialised equipment (a belt for you and a bungee-style line for your Goldie). Dogs must be 12 months old to compete, but you can start fitness training from around nine months and also teach all-important instructions, such as "haw" (left), "gee" (right), "steady" and Whoa!"

Agility

In this sport the dog completes an obstacle course under the guidance of his owner. You need a good element of control as the dog works off the lead.

In competition, each dog completes the course individually and is assessed on both time and

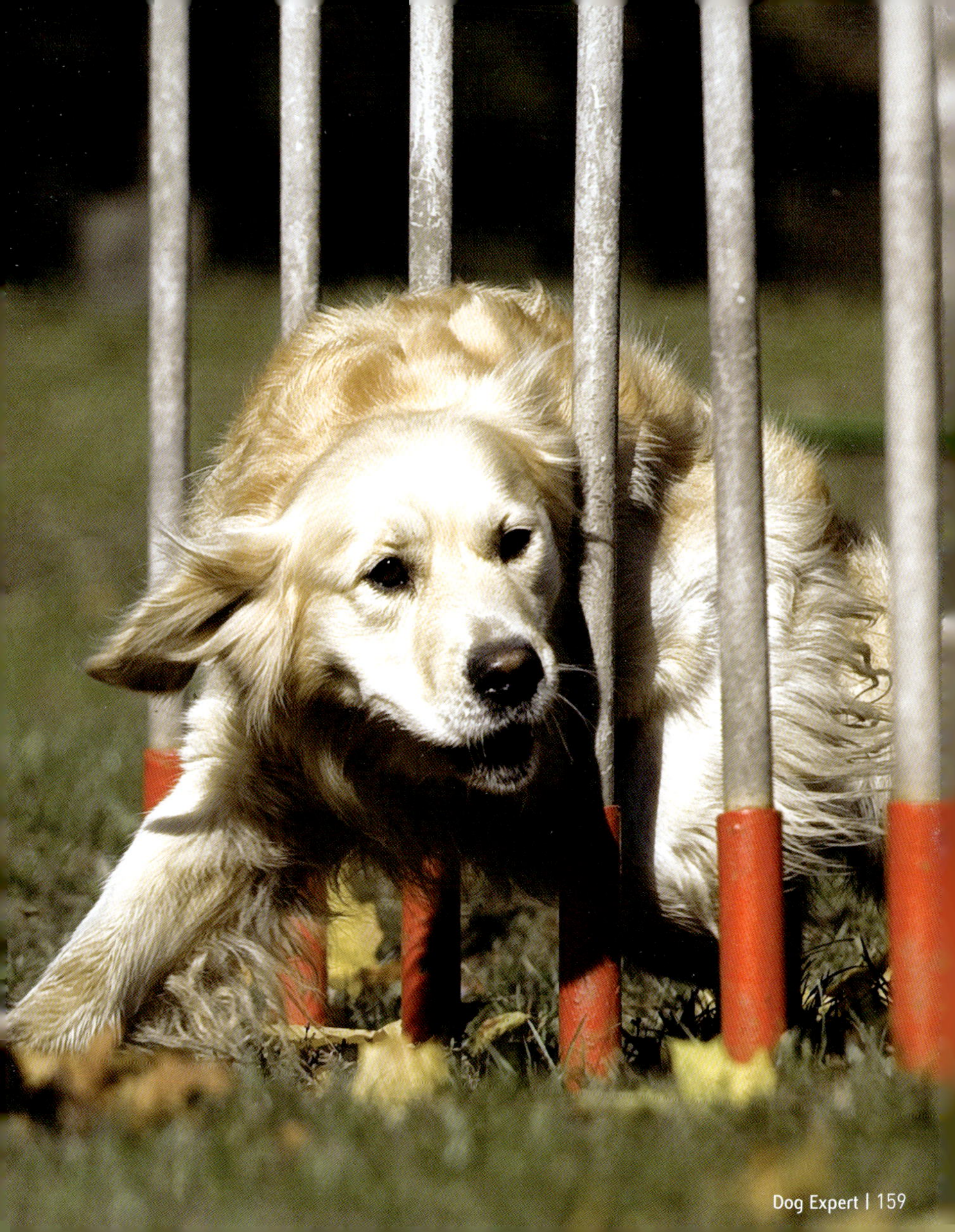

accuracy. The dog that completes the course with the fewest faults, in the fastest time, wins the class. The obstacles include an A-frame, a dog-walk, weaving poles, a seesaw, tunnels and jumps.

Showing

Exhibiting a dog in the show ring sounds easy but, in fact, it entails a lot of training and preparation. Your Golden Retriever will have to be calm and confident in the busy show atmosphere, so you need to work on his socialisation, and also take him to ringcraft classes so you both learn what is required in the ring. Your Goldie will be subjected to a detailed 'hands on' examination by the judge; he will need to stand still in a show pose and will also need to move on a loose lead so the judge can assess his gait.

Showing at the top level is highly addictive, so watch out; once you start, you will never have a free date in your diary!

Flyball

Flyball is a team sport; the dogs love it and it is undoubtedly the noisiest of all the canine sports! Four dogs are selected to run in a relay race against an opposing team. The dogs are sent out by their handlers to jump four hurdles, catch the ball from the flyball box and then return over the hurdles. At the top level, this sport is fast and furious and, although it is dominated by Border Collies, the Golden Retriever can make a big contribution.

Field trials

These are highly competitive, sometimes arduous, events over rough territory, held under Kennel Club rules to resemble a day's shooting in the field. Field Trial Golden Retrievers are expected to work with all manner of game, from rabbits and hares, to partridges and pheasants, and display their hunting ability and their obedience to commands.

Tracking

The Golden Retriever has an excellent sense of smell, so he is a good choice for this demanding sport where the dog must learn to follow scent trails of varying age, over different types of terrain. In the US, this is a sport in its own right; in the UK it is incorporated into Working Trials, where a dog must also compete in two other elements – control and agility.

Health care

We are fortunate that the Golden Retriever is a healthy dog and, with good routine care, a well-balanced diet, and sufficient exercise, most will experience few health problems.

However, it is your responsibility to put a programme of preventative health care in place – and this should start from the moment your puppy, or older dog, arrives in his new home.

Vaccinations

Dogs are subject to a number of contagious diseases. In the old days, these were killers, and resulted in heartbreak for many owners. Vaccinations have now been developed, and the occurrence of the major infectious diseases is now very rare. However, this will only remain the case if all pet owners follow a strict policy of vaccinating their dogs.

There are vaccinations available for the following diseases:

Dog Expert | 163

Adenovirus: (Canine Adenovirus): This affects the liver; affected dogs have a classic 'blue eye'.

Distemper: A viral disease which causes chest and gastro-intestinal damage. The brain may also be affected, leading to fits and paralysis.

Parvovirus: Causes severe gastro enteritis, and most commonly affects puppies.

Leptospirosis: This bacterial disease is carried by rats and affects many mammals, including humans. It causes liver and kidney damage.

Rabies: A virus that affects the nervous system and is invariably fatal. The first signs are abnormal behavior which may cause the infected dog to bite another animal or a person. Paralysis and death follow. Vaccination is compulsory in most countries. In the UK, dogs traveling overseas must be vaccinated.

Kennel Cough: There are several strains of Kennel Cough, but they all result in a harsh, dry, cough. This disease is rarely fatal; in fact most dogs make a good recovery within a matter of weeks and show few signs of ill health while they are affected. However, kennel cough is highly infectious among dogs that live together so, for this reason, most boarding kennels will insist that your dog is protected by the vaccine, which is given as nose drops.

Lyme disease: This is a bacterial disease transmitted by ticks (see page 170). The first signs are limping, but the heart, kidneys and nervous system can be affected. The ticks that transmit the disease occur in specific regions, such as the north-east states of the USA, some of the southern states, California and the upper Mississippi region. Lyme disease is still rare in the UK so vaccinations are not routinely offered.

Vaccination programme

In the USA, the American Animal Hospital Association advises vaccination for core diseases, which they list as: distemper, adenovirus, parvovirus and rabies. The requirement for vaccinating for non-core diseases – leptospirosis, lyme disease and kennel cough – should be assessed depending on a dog's individual risk and his likely exposure to the disease.

In the UK, vaccinations are routinely given for distemper, adenovirus, leptospirosis and parvovirus.

In most cases, a puppy will start his vaccinations at around eight weeks of age, with the second part given a fortnight later. However, this does vary depending on the individual policy of veterinary practices, and the incidence of disease in your area.

You should also talk to your vet about whether to give annual booster vaccinations. This depends on an individual dog's levels of immunity, and how long a particular vaccine remains effective.

Parasites

No matter how well you look after your Golden Retriever, you will have to accept that parasites – internal and external – are ever present, and you need to take preventative action.

Internal parasites: As the name suggests, these parasites live inside your dog. Most will find a home in the digestive tract, but there is also a parasite that lives in the heart. If infestation is unchecked, a dog's health will be severely jeopardised, but routine preventative treatment is simple and effective.

External parasites: These parasites live on your dog's body – in his skin and fur, and sometimes in his ears.

Roundworm

This is found in the small intestine, and signs of infestation will be a poor coat, a pot belly, diarrhoea and lethargy. Pregnant mothers should be treated, but it is almost inevitable that parasites will be passed on to the puppies. For this reason, a breeder will start a worming programme, which you will need to keep up.

Ask your vet for advice on treatment, which will need to continue throughout your dog's life.

Tapeworm

Infection occurs when fleas and lice are ingested; the adult worm takes up residence in the small intestine, releasing mobile segments (which contain eggs) which can be seen in a dog's faeces as small rice-like grains. The only other obvious sign of infestation is irritation of the anus. Again, routine preventative treatment is required throughout your Goldie's life.

Heartworm

This parasite is transmitted by mosquitoes, and so will only occur where these insects thrive. A warm environment is needed for the parasite to develop, so it is more likely to be present in areas with a warm, humid climate. However, it is found in all parts of the USA, although its prevalence does vary. At present, heartworm is rarely seen in the UK.

Heartworm live in the right side of the heart. Larvae can grow up to 14in (35cm) in length. A dog with heartworm is at severe risk from heart failure, so preventative treatment, as advised by your vet, is essential. Dogs living in the USA should have regular blood tests to check for the presence of infection.

Lungworm

Lungworm, or *Angiostrongylus vasorum*, is a parasite that lives in the heart and major blood vessels supplying the lungs. It can cause many problems, such as breathing difficulties, blood-clotting, sickness and diarrhoea, seizures, and can even be fatal. The parasite is carried by slugs and snails, and the dog becomes infected when ingesting these, often accidentally when rummaging through undergrowth. Lungworm is not common, but it is on the increase and a responsible owner should be aware of it. Fortunately, it is easily preventable and even affected dogs usually make a full recovery if treated early enough. Your vet will be able to advise you on the risks in your area and what form of treatment may be required.

Fleas

A dog may carry dog fleas, cat fleas, and even human fleas. The flea stays on the dog only long enough to have a blood meal and to breed, but its presence will result in itching and scratching. If your dog has an allergy to fleas – which is usually a reaction to the flea's saliva – he will scratch himself until he is raw.

Spot-on treatment, which should be administered on a routine basis, is easy to use and highly effective on all types of fleas. You can also treat your dog with a spray or with insecticidal shampoo. Bear in mind that the whole environment your dog lives in will need to be sprayed, and all other pets living in your home will also need to be treated.

How to detect fleas

You may suspect your dog has fleas, but how can you be sure? There are two methods to try.

Run a fine comb through your dog's coat, and see if you can detect the presence of fleas on the skin, or clinging to the comb. Alternatively, sit your dog on white paper and rub his back. This will dislodge faeces from the fleas, which will be visible as small brown specks. To double check, shake the specks on to damp cotton-wool (cotton). Flea faeces consists of the dried blood taken from the host, so if the specks turn a lighter shade of red, you know your dog has fleas.

Ticks

These are blood-sucking parasites which are most frequently found in rural areas where sheep or deer are present. The main danger is their ability to pass lyme disease to both dogs and humans. Lyme disease is prevalent in some areas of the USA (see page 165), although it is still rare in the UK. The treatment you give your dog for fleas generally works for ticks, but you should discuss the best product to use with your vet.

How to remove a tick

If you spot a tick on your dog, do not try to pluck it off as you risk leaving the hard mouth parts embedded in his skin. The best way to remove a tick is to use a fine pair of tweezers, or you can buy a tick remover. Grasp the tick head firmly and then pull the tick straight out from the skin. If you are using a tick remover, check the instructions, as some recommend a circular twist when pulling. When you have removed the tick, clean the area with mild soap and water.

Ear mites

These parasites live in the outer ear canal. The signs of infestation are a brown, waxy discharge, and your dog will continually shake his head and scratch his ear. If you suspect your Golden Retriever has ear mites, a visit to the vet will be need so that medicated ear drops can be prescribed.

Fur mites

These small, white parasites are visible to the naked eye and are often referred to as 'walking dandruff'. They cause a scurfy coat and mild itchiness. However, they are zoonetic – transferable to humans – so prompt treatment with an insecticide prescribed by your vet is essential.

Harvest mites

These are picked up from the undergrowth, and can be seen as a bright orange patch on the webbing between the toes, although this can be found elsewhere on the body, such as on the ears flaps. Treatment is effective with the appropriate insecticide.

Skin mites

There are two types of parasite that burrow into a dog's skin. *Demodex canis* is transferred from a mother to her pups while they are feeding. Treatment is with a topical preparation, and sometimes antibiotics are needed.

The other skin mite is *Sarcoptes scabiei,* which causes intense itching and hair loss. It is highly contagious, so all dogs in a household will need to be treated, which involves repeated bathing with a medicated shampoo.

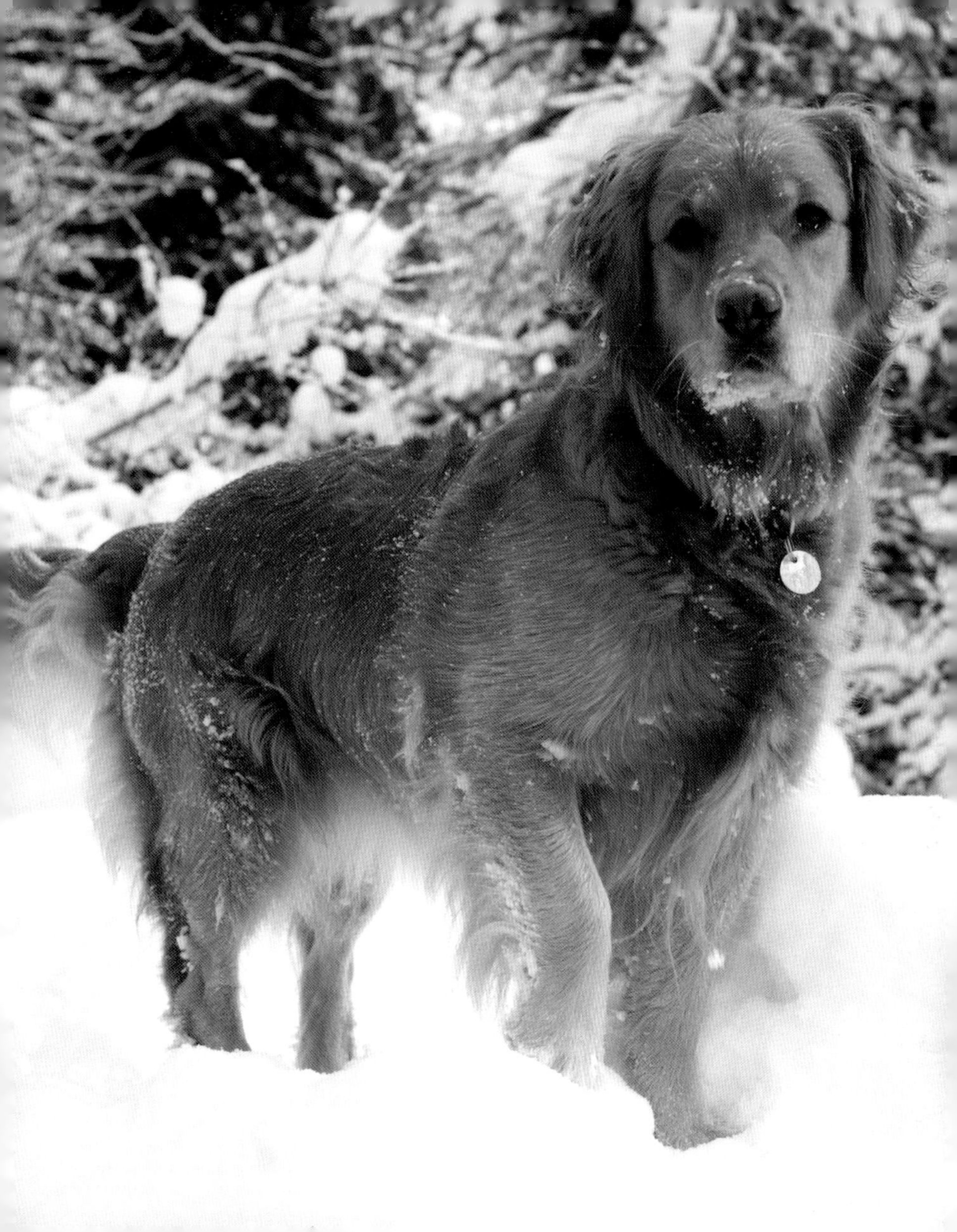

Common ailments

As with all living animals, dogs can be affected by a variety of ailments. Most can be treated effectively after consulting with your vet, who will prescribe appropriate medication and will advise you on how to care for your dog's needs.

Here are some of the more common problems that could affect your Golden Retriever, with advice on how to deal with them.

Anal glands

These are two small sacs on either side of the anus, which produce a dark-brown secretion which dogs use when they mark their territory. The anal glands should empty every time a dog defecates but if they become blocked or impacted, a dog will experience increasing discomfort. He may nibble at his rear end,

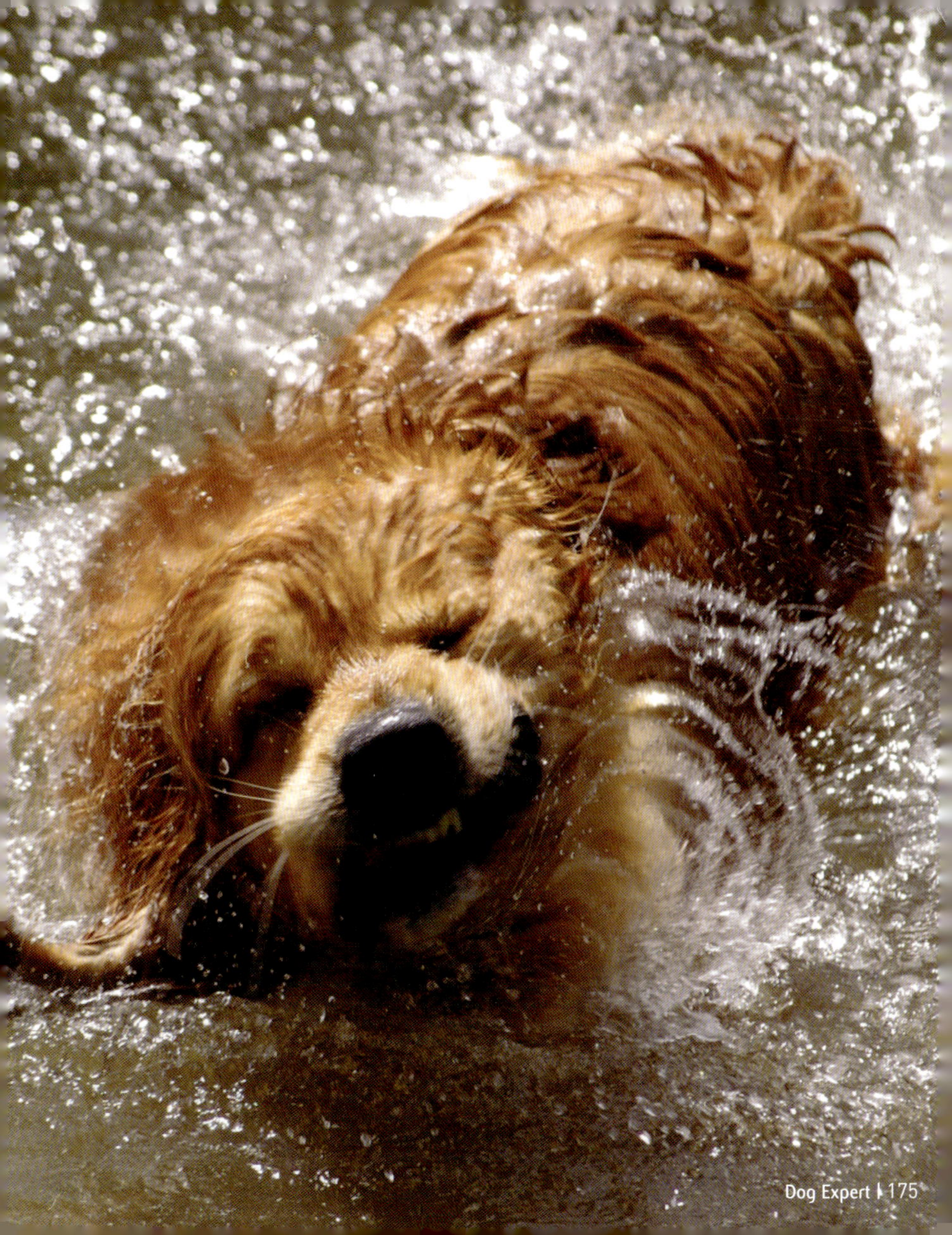

or 'scoot' his bottom along the ground to relieve the irritation.

Treatment involves a trip to the vet where the glands will be emptied manually. It is important to do this without delay or infection may occur.

Dental problems

Good dental hygiene will do much to minimise gum infection and tooth decay. If tartar accumulates to the extent that you cannot remove it by brushing, the vet will need to intervene. In a situation such as this, an anaesthetic will need to be administered so the tartar can be removed manually.

Diarrhoea

There are many reasons why a dog has diarrhoea, but most commonly it is the result of scavenging – a common problem with Golden Retrievers – a sudden change of diet, or an adverse reaction to a particular type of food.

If your dog is suffering from diarrhoea, the first step is to withdraw food for a day. It is important that he does not dehydrate, so make sure that fresh drinking water is available. However, drinking too much can increase the diarrhoea, which may be accompanied with vomiting, so limit how much he drinks at any one time.

After allowing the stomach to rest, feed a bland diet, such as white fish or chicken with boiled rice, for a few days. In most cases, your dog's motions will return to normal and you can resume normal feeding, although this should be done gradually.

However, if this fails to work and the diarrhoea persists for more than a few days, you should consult you vet. Your dog may have an infection which needs to be treated with antibiotics, or the diarrhoea may indicate some other problem which needs expert diagnosis.

Ear infections

The Golden Retriever has drop ears that lie close to his head, which increases the risk of ear infections.

A healthy ear is clean with no sign of redness or inflammation, and no evidence of a waxy brown discharge or a foul odor. If you see your dog scratching his ear, shaking his head, or holding one ear at an odd angle, you will need to consult your vet. The most likely causes are ear mites, an infection, or there may a foreign body, such as a grass seed, trapped in the ear.

Depending on the cause, treatment is with medicated ear drops, possibly containing antibiotics. If a foreign body is suspected, the vet will need to carry our further investigations.

Eye problems

The Golden Retriever has medium-sized eyes, with tight rims; they are set well apart and deep in the sockets so they are not vulnerable to injury as can be the case with breeds such as the Pug, that have protruding eyes.

If your Goldie's eyes look red and sore, he may be suffering from conjunctivitis. This may, or may not be accompanied with a watery or a crusty discharge. Conjunctivitis can be caused by a bacterial or viral infection, it could be the result of an injury, an adverse reaction to pollen, or a congenital defect, see Ectropion, page 184.

You will need to consult your vet for a correct diagnosis, but in the case of an infection, treatment with medicated eye drops is effective.

Foreign bodies

In the home, puppies – and some older dogs – cannot resist chewing anything that looks interesting. This is particularly true of Golden Retrievers – a very 'mouthy' breed. It is therefore essential that the toys you choose for your dog should be suitably robust to withstand damage. But bear in mind that children's toys may prove irresistible, and some dogs will chew – and swallow

– anything from socks, tights, and other items from the laundry basket to golf balls and stones from the garden. Obviously, these items are indigestible and could cause an obstruction in your dog's intestine, which is potentially lethal.

The signs to look for are vomiting, and a tucked up posture. The dog will often be restless and will look as though he is in pain.

In this situation, you must get your dog to the vet without delay as surgery will be needed to remove the obstruction.

Heatstroke

The Golden Retriever's head structure is without exaggeration, which means that he has a straightforward respiratory system.

However, all dogs are vulnerable to overheating in hot weather. If the weather is warm make sure your Goldie always has access to shady areas, and wait for a cooler part of the day before going for a walk. Be extra careful if you leave your dog in the car, as the temperature can rise dramatically - even on a cloudy day. Heatstroke can happen very rapidly, and unless you are able lower your dog's temperature, it can be fatal.

If your Golden Retriever appears to be suffering from heatstroke, lie him flat and work at lowering his temperature by spraying him with cool water and covering him with wet towels. As soon as he has made some recovery, take him to the vet where cold intravenous fluids can be administered.

Lameness/limping

There are a wide variety of reasons why a dog can go lame from a simple muscle strain, to a fracture, ligament damage, or more complex problems with the joints. If you are concerned about your dog, do not delay in seeking help.

As your Golden Retriever becomes more elderly, he

may suffer from arthritis, which you will see as general stiffness, particularly when he gets up after resting. It will help if you ensure his bed is in a warm draught-free location, and if he gets wet after exercise, you must dry him thoroughly.

If you Goldie seems to be in pain, consult your vet who will be able to help with pain relief medication.

Skin problems

If your dog is scratching or nibbling at his skin, first check he is free from fleas. There are other external parasites which cause itching and hair loss, but you will need a vet to help you find the culprit.

An allergic reaction can cause major skin problems, but it can be quite an undertaking to find the cause of the allergy. You will need to follow your vet's advice, which often requires eliminating specific ingredients from the diet, as well as looking at environmental factors.

Breed-specific disorders

Like all pedigree dogs, the Golden Retriever does have a few breed-related disorders. If diagnosed with any of the diseases listed below, it is important to remember that they can affect offspring, so breeding from affected dogs should be discouraged.

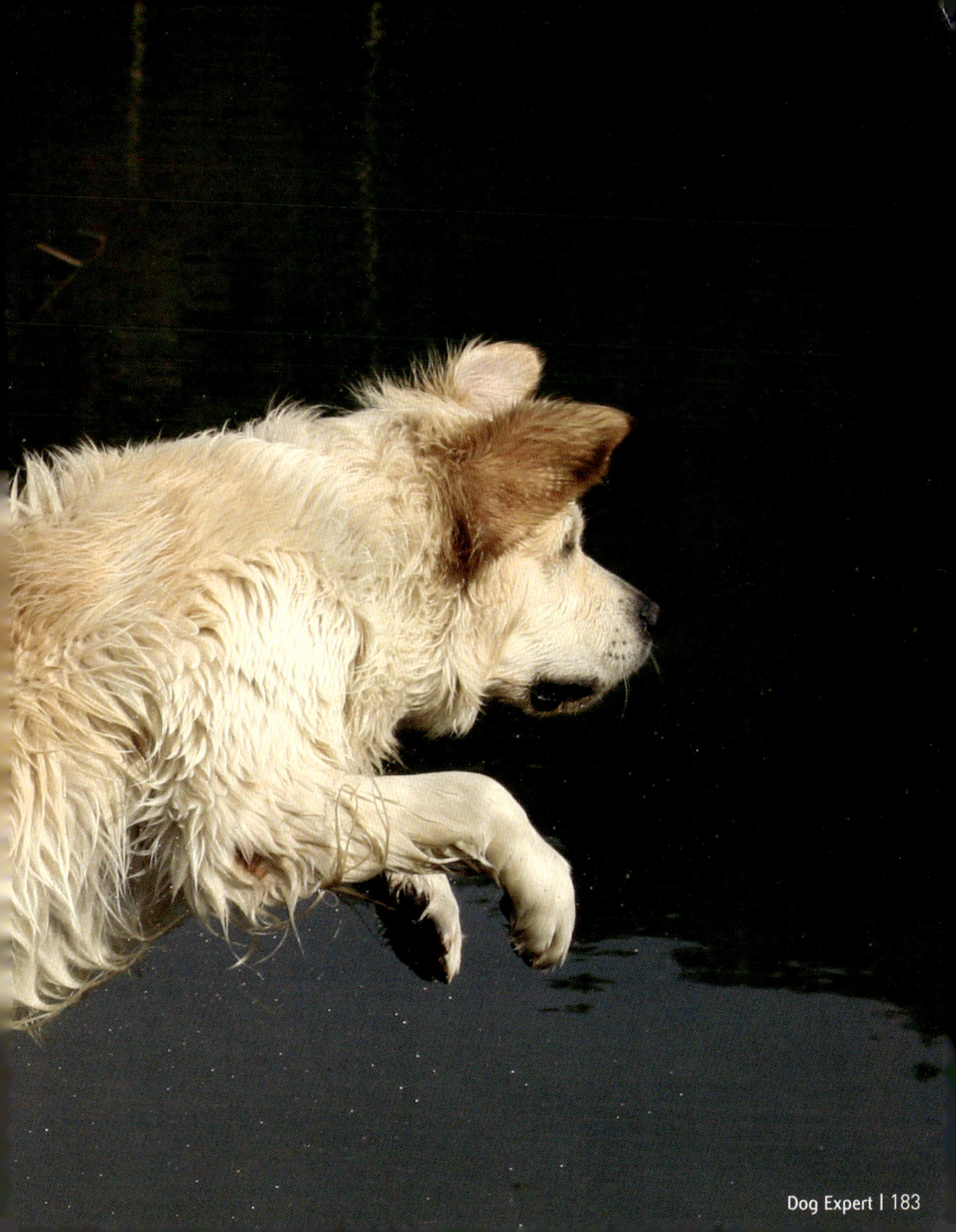

DNA testing

There are now recognised screening tests to enable breeders to check for affected individuals and hence reduce the prevalence of these diseases within the breed. DNA testing is also becoming more widely available, and as research into the different genetic diseases progresses, more DNA tests are being developed.

Epilepsy

It is thought that this condition is inherited; it is often first seen in adolescent and young dogs, aged between six months and three years. Fits may occur singly or in clusters. There is no cure but medication can help to control the fits.

Eye disorders

Golden Retrievers can be affected by a number of eye disorders. Testing is carried out by the Canine Eye Registration Foundation in the US; in the UK there is a combined scheme run by the British Veterinary Association, the Kennel Club and the International Sheep Dog Society.

Ectropion

This is a condition where the eyelids roll outwards

which can result in conjunctivitis. However, it often resolves as the dog matures and corrective surgery is rarely necessary.

Entropion

This is where the eyelids roll inwards, which is more serious as it can result in damage to the eyeball. Surgery is reasonably straightforward and effective.

Hereditary cataracts

Cataracts are an opacification of the lens that tends to occur in older dogs. Golden Retrievers suffer from hereditary cataracts where the lens is often affected in younger dogs, although the condition may also be seen later in life. There are varying degrees of severity. The inherited form often has little effect on eyesight but, if necessary, surgery is usually successful.

Retinal defects

There are a number of conditions in this category, which include General Progressive Retinal Atrophy (GPRA), Central Progressive Retinal Atrophy (CPRA), and Multifocal Retinal Dysplasia (MRD).

It is essential that all breeding stock have the appropriate eye tests, and there is also a DNA blood test to determine if dogs are likely to be affected, or are carriers of the defective gene.

Elbow dysplasia

Also known as Elbow Osteochondrosis, this is often first seen as forelimb lameness is adolescent Golden Retrievers. It is a progressive, degenerative joint disease. Breeding stock should have their elbows X-rayed and scored under the OFA scheme in the US and the BVA/KC scheme in the UK.

Hip dysplasia (Hd)

This is where the ball-and-socket joint of the hip develops incorrectly so that the head of the femur (ball) and the acetabulum of the pelvis (socket) do not fit snugly. This causes pain in the joint and may be seen as lameness in dogs as young as five months old with deterioration into severe arthritis over time.

In the US, hip scoring is carried out by the Orthopaedic Foundation for Animals. X-rays are submitted when a dog is two years old, categorised as Normal (Excellent, Good, Fair), Borderline, and Dysplastic (Mild, Moderate, Severe). The hip grades of Excellent, Good and Fair are within normal limits and are given OFA numbers.

In the UK, the minimum age for the hips to be assessed by X-ray is 12 months. Each hip can score from a possible perfect 0 to a deformed 53. Both left and right scores are added together to give the total hip score.

Muscular dystrophy (canine)

This is linked to the X chromosome so it tends to occur in male dogs. Females may carry the gene without being outwardly affected. The condition mirrors the human form of the disease, which involves muscular weakness and degeneration.

Tricuspid valve defect (TVD)

This is a congenital heart defect where an affected dog is born with a malformed heart valve between the two chambers of the right side of the heart. This ranges in severity from a slight malformation, which has little effect on life expectancy, to a leaky valve which leads to congestive heart failure in young dogs.

The condition may be detected when a vet listens to the heart with a stethoscope, which is part of the health check given to a puppy prior to starting a vaccination course. A detailed ultrasound examination is then required to discover the extent of the problem.

Summing up

It may give the pet owner cause for concern to find about health problems that may affect their dog. But it is important to bear in mind that acquiring some basic knowledge is an asset, as it will allow you to spot signs of trouble at an early stage. Early diagnosis is very often the means to the most effective treatment.

Fortunately, the Golden Retriever is generally a healthy and disease-free dog with his only visits to the vet being annual check-ups. In most cases, owners can look forward to enjoying many happy years with this outstanding companion.

Useful addresses

Breed & Kennel Clubs
Please contact your Kennel Club to obtain contact information about breed clubs in your area.

UK
The Kennel Club (UK)
1 Clarges Street London, W1J 8AB
Telephone: 0870 606 6750
Fax: 0207 518 1058
Web: www.thekennelclub.org.uk

USA
American Kennel Club (AKC)
5580 Centerview Drive, Raleigh, NC 27606.
Telephone: 919 233 9767
Fax: 919 233 3627
Email: info@akc.org
Web: www.akc.org

United Kennel Club (UKC)
100 E Kilgore Rd, Kalamazoo,
MI 49002-5584, USA.
Tel: 269 343 9020
Fax: 269 343 7037
Web: www.ukcdogs.com/

Australia
Australian National Kennel Council (ANKC)
The Australian National Kennel Council is the administrative body for pure breed canine affairs in Australia. It does not, however, deal directly with dog exhibitors, breeders or judges. For information pertaining to breeders, clubs or shows, please contact the relevant State or Territory Body.

International
Fédération Cynologique Internationalé (FCI)
Place Albert 1er, 13, B-6530 Thuin, Belgium.
Tel: +32 71 59.12.38
Fax: +32 71 59.22.29
Web: www.fci.be/

Training and behavior
UK
Association of Pet Dog Trainers
Telephone: 01285 810811
Web: http://www.apdt.co.uk

Canine Behaviour
Association of Pet Behaviour Counsellors
Telephone: 01386 751151
Web: http://www.apbc.org.uk/

USA
Association of Pet Dog Trainers
Tel: 1 800 738 3647
Web: www.apdt.com/

American College of Veterinary Behaviorists
Web: http://dacvb.org/

American Veterinary Society of Animal Behavior
Web: www.avsabonline.org/

Australia
APDT Australia Inc
Web: www.apdt.com.au

For details of regional behaviorists, contact the relevant State or Territory Controlling Body.

Activities

UK
Agility Club
http://www.agilityclub.co.uk/

British Flyball Association
Telephone: 01628 829623
Web: http://www.flyball.org.uk/

USA
North American Dog Agility Council
Web: www.nadac.com/

North American Flyball Association, Inc.
Tel/Fax: 800 318 6312
Web: www.flyball.org/

Australia
Agility Dog Association of Australia
Tel: 0423 138 914
Web: www.adaa.com.au/

NADAC Australia
Web: www.nadacaustralia.com/

Australian Flyball Association
Tel: 0407 337 939
Web: www.flyball.org.au/

International
World Canine Freestyle Organisation
Tel: (718) 332-8336
Web: www.worldcaninefreestyle.org

Health

UK
British Small Animal Veterinary Association
Tel: 01452 726700
Web: http://www.bsava.com/

Royal College of Veterinary Surgeons
Tel: 0207 222 2001
Web: www.rcvs.org.uk

www.dogbooksonline.co.uk/healthcare/

Alternative Veterinary Medicine Centre
Tel: 01367 710324
Web: www.alternativevet.org/

USA
American Veterinary Medical Association
Tel: 800 248 2862
Web: www.avma.org

American College of Veterinary Surgeons
Tel: 301 916 0200
Toll Free: 877 217 2287
Web: www.acvs.org/

Canine Eye Registration Foundation
The Veterinary Medical DataBases
1717 Philo Rd, PO Box 3007,
Urbana, IL 61803-3007
Tel: 217-693-4800
Fax: 217-693-4801
Web: http://www.vmdb.org/cerf.html

Orthopaedic Foundation of Animals
2300 E Nifong Boulevard
Columbia, Missouri, 65201-3806
Tel: 573 442-0418
Fax: 573 875-5073
Web: http://www.offa.org/

American Holistic Veterinary Medical Association
Tel: 410 569 0795
Web: www.ahvma.org/

Australia
Australian Small Animal Veterinary Association
Tel: 02 9431 5090
Web: www.asava.com.au

Australian Veterinary Association
Tel: 02 9431 5000
Web: www.ava.com.au

Australian College Veterinary Scientists
Tel: 07 3423 2016
Web: http://acvsc.org.au

Australian Holistic Vets
Web: www.ahv.com.au/